Hudson River

An Historic and Scenic Natural Treasure

by
John Bernardo

HERITAGE BOOKS
2013

HERITAGE BOOKS
AN IMPRINT OF HERITAGE BOOKS, INC.

Books, CDs, and more—Worldwide

For our listing of thousands of titles see our website at
www.HeritageBooks.com

Published 2013 by
HERITAGE BOOKS, INC.
Publishing Division
5810 Ruatan Street
Berwyn Heights, Md. 20740

Copyright © 2013 John Bernardo

All rights reserved. No part of this book may be reproduced or transmitted in any form or by any means, electronic or mechanical, including photocopying, recording or by any information storage and retrieval system without written permission from the author, except for the inclusion of brief quotations in a review.

International Standard Book Numbers
Paperbound: 978-0-7884-5521-6
Clothbound: 978-0-7884-9054-5

Table of Contents

Preface   v
     Introduction to Author and Book

Hudson River: 9
     Overview of the Hudson River and Its Tributaries

Chapter 1:   21
     Aquatic Plants, Habitats, Hudson River Estuaries (tributaries within the estuaries), Its Ecosystem, Fish and Wildlife

Chapter 2:   41
     Hudson Estuary Program, Its Ecosystem (including changes in it), Fish and other Wildlife (Con't) /River Pollution Problems & Solutions

Photo Section   63

Chapter 3:   81
     Hudson River Access/Transportation Links (Railroads, Recreation and Commercial Vessels, Bridges, Tunnels, etc.)

Chapter 4:   93
     Hudson River Historical Attractions/Recreational Activities and Sites

Chapter 5:   121
     Newly Completed & Future Hudson Riverfront Development Projects and Hudson River Real Estate Market

Chapter 6:   135
     Some Historical Highlights of the Hudson River and Its Valley

Author's Summary: 145

John Bernardo
Author

Preface
John Bernardo - Hudson River

Writing has been my passion since 1988 when I became a freelance journalist. So far, I have written over 500 (non-fiction) articles. Some of those stories were published in newspapers; the rest in magazines. In addition to my articles, I am the proud, published author of five books. Of course, *Hudson River* represents my most recent, published book.

In July 2001, I became the published author of *What You Can Do For Your Own Flying Safety & Security*, a non-fiction book. In April 2003, I became the co-author of another non-fiction book titled, *Airline Safety: The Passenger's Role*. In July 2003, I became the author of a fiction book titled: *The River*, an adventure book geared toward children and young adult readers. In January, 2013, I became the author of another non-fiction book titled: *Delaware River*.

What inspired me to write about the Hudson River was *The River* book I wrote and the village of Dobbs Ferry in New York State (located near the Hudson) where I was raised. My keen interest in rivers, mountains, and nature also motivated me to write about this famous river. In fact, when I did research on the Hudson River, I was able to get a wealth of information on the subject. I then soon found out that the information I could obtain on the Hudson seemed like it would never end. However, the Hudson River has a mouth and it ends. Hence, I came to a point where I had to finish my book on the Hudson River, which I feel, is a fascinating river. My book educates readers on the Hudson River's plants, ecology, fish, wildlife, geology, geography, transportation, recreation, real estate (includes riverside parks and other developments), the river's tributaries, and its history.

As for myself, I was born and raised in Mount Vernon, New York. Mount Vernon is a city in Westchester County that lies just north of the Bronx in New York City. Then when I was twelve years old, my family and I relocated to a small village called Dobbs Ferry, which is about twenty miles north of New York City.

Dobbs Ferry is located along the Hudson where the river is brackish (part freshwater, part salt-water).

Every summer, from the time I was twelve until I turned eighteen, my younger brother, Joe Bernardo, and I regularly fished and crabbed at Dobbs Ferry's Waterfront Park on the Hudson River. And from scenic, vantage points on Waterfront Park on a clear day, Joe and I were able to look downriver and see the Statue of Liberty and New York Harbor.

Without a doubt, Joe was the better fisherman than I. And regardless if the river was at high or low tide or if its currents were calm or rough, he would reel in many eel, catfish, and striped bass. I would also pull in some fish during those hot months of June, July, and August, but I couldn't keep up with my brother.

Besides fishing, Joe and I threw out metal crab traps in the Hudson (we used freshwater sunfish for bait) and pulled the traps back to shore about every twenty to thirty minutes. Both of us did well during those steamy, summer months and at least each hour, we pulled in two to three male blue crabs. Sometimes female crabs got tangled in our traps, but we immediately threw the females back into the river. It is illegal for anyone to keep females because that has a negative impact on the Hudson's blue crab population. On a typical day of crabbing, Joe and I caught around a half-dozen or more blue crabs. Once caught, we brought the males home to dump the shellfish out of our buckets and into a pot of boiling water. After a minute or so, the crabs would die in the boiling water and then we used nutcrackers to crack open their body parts (which included their claws) and ate the crabmeat. The crabs tasted good and so did the striped bass, eel and catfish that we reeled in from the Hudson.

In addition to fishing and crabbing, my family and I traveled on a big cruise ship, *The Hudson Dayliner*, when I was twelve on the Hudson River. The "new" *Dayliner* transported us from New York City (New York Harbor in Manhattan) to Bear Mountain and West Point Military Academy in upstate New York. That was a scenic trip on the Hudson that I will never forget. It was a time when we had stunning views of the Hudson (a unique, scenic, mighty, and historic river) and its shoreline.

The main purpose of my book is twofold. First and foremost, it educates readers on the importance of the Hudson

River as a natural resource, key transportation artery, and chief provider of food, oxygen, and water needed to sustain our local, national, and global ecosystem. Second, my book mentions its characteristics, tributaries, and how the river is an historic and scenic treasure. A treasure that also economically benefits New York and New Jersey by offering its residents and tourists many attractions and recreational opportunities.

Moreover, after you read my book, *Hudson River*, you will get a general idea of what the geology of the river and its shoreline is like and how the Hudson enhances the lifestyle of Hudson Valley and northern New Jersey residents. Unlike other authors who have written books on their sailboat trip experiences or have focused on a particular aspect of the Hudson River, my book gives readers the tools they need to understand the river from a variety of qualities that make up this special waterway. By far, the Hudson can't be described just by its history or by what fish anglers reel in each summer. There are many benefits the river provides to our ecosystem, economy and ourselves that can't be described just over some author's fishing or hiking trip along the Hudson Valley. In addition, I think readers will agree that the timing of my book couldn't have been better. My book, *Hudson River*, comes out at a time that coincides with September 2009, the date when many people observed the 400th Anniversary of Henry Hudson's discovery of the river.

Moreover, writing about the Hudson River does educate readers on the subject; however, it doesn't give them a sense of the natural scenery that makes the river special. That is why I'm thanking Carl Heilman, a photographer in upstate New York, for his contribution to my book. Heilman's pictures truly depict the unique, breathtaking scenery of the Hudson that has attracted many artists, writers, tourists and others to the Upper Hudson Estuary and Adirondack Mountains Region.

I'm also dedicating *Hudson River* to history buffs, nature advocates, river lovers and to good fishermen (that include my brother, Joe). A special dedication goes out to my daughters, Michelle and Melissa Bernardo, who like myself, find rivers, river fish and wildlife by rivers interesting. We appreciate and enjoy waterways, like the Hudson River, because rivers provide habitats for a variety of life forms and benefit the quality of life for different civilizations.

Hudson River
(Overview of the Hudson & Its Tributaries)

The Hudson River estuary (an arm of the sea at the lower end of a river) is one of New York's outstanding natural resources, world renowned for its history and scenery. The Hudson is also an important ecological and cultural river that represents a vital part of the Atlantic coast ecosystem. The Hudson River is regionally significant as a productive estuary (a water passage where the tide meets a river current) and the Hudson is one of only a few tidal rivers on the North Atlantic coast of the United States. Excluding the St. Lawrence and Niagara Rivers on the northern border of the state, the Hudson River is New York's largest river, with a watershed that totals 13,390 square miles or 28% of New York State. About 25% of the Hudson River Basin is geared toward agriculture, 60% is forest and 8% is urban.

The Hudson River symbolizes Eastern New York State. It is New York's longest river running 315 miles as it originates in several postglacial lakes in the Adirondack Mountains near Mt. Marcy (the Adirondack's highest mountain where its elevation is at 5,344 ft.). The tiny Lake Tear of the Clouds is regarded as the original source of its main headstream, the Opalescent River (the Hudson's origin wasn't declared until the 1870s). A series of dams and locks maintains navigability on the upper reaches of the Hudson River and provides access to the St. Lawrence Seaway and Great Lakes via Lake Chaplain. Recreational boats sometimes traverse New York on the Erie Canal that joins the Hudson River via the Mohawk River (a main Hudson tributary).

From the Adirondacks the Hudson flows south through its 10-to-20-mile-wide valley and then through seven locks, over fifteen dams and three waterfalls before it finally runs out at its mouth located in the Atlantic Ocean (New York Harbor area). In fact, the Hudson River is tidal for over half its length for 150 miles up to Troy, NY. Unlike other rivers, the Hudson has strong tides, currents and waves and as a result, no deltas (fanlike deposits at the river's end) were created. Instead, the Hudson has a drowned mouth (estuary). During the last Ice Age, glaciers thousands of feet thick gouged the river's bed to below sea level. As the glaciers retreated about 18,000 years ago, the Atlantic Ocean's waters rose and poured in behind them, mingling with fresh water from the Hudson's newly thawed tributaries to create the river we know of today. Thus, the lowest portions of the river were submerged.

The river drains New York and sections of Vermont, Massachusetts, Connecticut and New Jersey. The Hudson River Basin is comprised of three areas: the upper Hudson from Mt. Marcy to Troy, NY, the Mohawk River (its tributary) from Rome, NY to Troy, and the lower Hudson from Troy to the New York Harbor. The Hudson and Mohawk basins are freshwater; the lower Hudson is an estuary, with water greater than one practical salinity unit (psu) normally below West Point, NY.

Regarding other components of the Hudson, its deepest point is located at World's End near West Point in the Highlands (upstate New York) which is 216 feet deep. Its widest point is at Haverstraw Bay, NY where it is three and one half miles wide. Haverstraw Bay also is composed of much shallow water which takes in a lot of sunlight, energizing the growth of plankton (tiny drifting organisms). In the spring, the area's warmer waters allow phytoplankton (plankton capable of photosynthesis) to grow rapidly, providing food for very small drifting animals (zooplankton). A huge amount of zooplankton in the shallows of Haverstraw makes it an ideal nursery location for hungry newborn fish.

And as the Hudson River continues to pass different points along its path, it flows almost entirely within New York State, the exception being its final segment, where it forms the boundary between New York and northeastern New Jersey for 21 miles. The New York State Barge Canal system links the Hudson to the Great Lakes and Lake Champlain. The Richelieu Canal connects it with the St. Lawrence River.

The Hudson provides a significant recreational fishery and outlet for New York State residents and at its lower portion, New Jersey, it's the vital waterway needed for barge transportation between the Atlantic Ocean and the Great Lakes. The river is also a source of drinking water for communities in New York that include the village of Rhinebeck, Highland, Poughkeepsie, East Fishkill, Port Ewen and part of Hyde Park. In addition, New York City has long-term plans to use the Hudson River as a backup water supply to its vast watersheds that consist of much of the Catskill Mountains. Millions of more people depend on the river for drinking water indirectly, via the creeks, streams, and groundwater that are connected to the Hudson.

Within the Hudson Valley, warm summers and relatively cold winters characterize its climate. The average temperatures in the region exceed 75 degrees F during July and August and drop to 28 F in January and February.

During the winter, the upper Hudson Valley receives about 60 inches of snowfall while the lower valley typically gets about 40 inches. Snowfall normally happens between mid-December and mid-March. During hot summer days, temperatures could reach 90 F. By the end of the summer, the water temperature is normally about 72 degrees F. On average, the valley gets about two to three inches of rain per month. Rainfall in the area is fairly distributed evenly throughout the year, with an average value of 46 inches/year. Rainfall is continuous throughout the summer when the freshwater flow rates in the estuary are minimum. Severe droughts are rare but there are occasional periods of below average rainfall. Besides rainwater, humidity affects the region's climate during the summertime. In June, daily average relative humidity reaches 73 % and remains uniform between 70% and 73% throughout the summer. There are occasionally intervals of humid conditions with temperatures reaching the 90s yet temperatures tend to be cooler in the mountains of Catskill Park. From June through September, the Hudson Valley experiences about 60 to 70 % of possible sunshine hours. In addition to rain, seasonal temperatures and humidity, wind conditions affect the area's climate throughout the year and are influenced by local valley topography. Above the river and beneath the high ridges, the wind direction tends to head upstream during the day and downstream at night.

Regarding future climatic conditions, the Hudson River, like any other waterway in the world, can be affected by global warming. Scientists state that the health of the Hudson is still threatened. The warming of the planet could flood coastal areas and harmful species transported from other continents could ruin the river's intricate and sensitive web of life. Scientists point out that regarding global warming, no other threat has the potential to upend the Hudson River ecosystem like climate change. In fact, according to the "Climate Change and a Global City" study, melting ice caps could make water in the Hudson River estuary rise between four and twelve inches by 2020 and 9.5 to 42.5 inches by 2080. The wide-ranging impacts include a northward migration of brackish water, threatening water supplies including Poughkeepsie's, and more frequent flooding of low-lying areas (such as marshes, wetlands & commuter train tracks) that are important habitats for birds, fish and other wildlife.

Yet despite possible threats from global warming, today the Hudson River still maintains its uniqueness due it has a dynamic character. From Troy, NY south to the river's mouth in New York Harbor, the Hudson takes on the properties of the ocean as well as a river. While the northern half of the river is freshwater fed by groundwater, snowmelt and rain, the southern estuary section is a tidal mix of salty seawater and freshwater.

North and above the Federal Dam at Troy, NY, the Hudson River has a conventional river flow, with a series of streams and rivers feeding from western and eastern uplands into the main course of the river; yet below the dam, the river is tidal.

Depending upon the movement of the tide, the river flows opposite ways. Without question, tides define the river's character, as the Mohican Indians recognized the river when they called it 'Muhheakunnuk,' which means "great waters constantly in motion." A Native American name for the Hudson was "Shattemuc" meaning "River That Flows Both Ways." The Algonquin Indians referred to the Hudson as "River Which Flows Two Ways." Due to its tides, different names of the river had derived through the years. Yet for the most part, the Hudson River is a drowned river and symbolizes an open book to the earth's history.

The entire length of the Hudson is affected by tides. The highest tide in the river (4.7-ft.) occurs in Troy, its northernmost point (West Point in the Hudson Highlands) only sees a 2.7-foot rise. The northern half of the river also flows from north to south and from high ground to low ground, the southern estuary stretch has been known to flow both ways because of tidal influence. In the Hudson every six hours the tides will shift pushing water into the river mouth on a flood tide and pulling water back out the mouth on an ebb tide. The difference in elevation between high and low tides creates tidal currents. The timing of these currents mimics the rise and fall of the tides. Inclement weather, such as strong winds or excessive rains, can impact the currents by overwhelming or suppressing them. In some areas on the river, change in watercolor can reflect the current.

The influence of currents and tides on the Hudson River varies depending upon location. For instance, from Troy, NY to Manhattan there is no drop at all in the surface elevation of the river. But at the dam in Troy, the rise and fall of ocean tides and the mixture of fresh and salt water influence the river. The tidal Hudson begins as fresh water in Troy, gradually turns brackish near the Hudson Highlands and becomes noticeably salty at the Tappan Zee Bridge (which goes over the river connecting Tarrytown in Westchester County, NY with Nyack in Rockland County, NY).

The river is also home to the Hudson River Reserve, which is a network of four coastal wetlands located along 100 miles of the Hudson Estuary in New York State. The natural, scenic beauty of the Hudson Valley earned the Hudson River the nickname "America's Rhine," comparing it to that of the popular forty-mile stretch of Germany's Rhine River Valley between the cities of Koblenz and Bingen. The valley of the Hudson is an important flyway for migratory birds and is home to many threatened and endangered species such as the bald eagle and heartleaf plantain.

Indeed the Hudson Valley is well known within the New York State region and perhaps throughout the world. However, deep below the Hudson's surface lies the old river channel, stretching from the Adirondacks out into the Atlantic Ocean where it drops over the edge of the continental shelf and into the vast Hudson Canyon. Unlike the river's valley, many people may not be aware of the Hudson Canyon; but nonetheless, the Hudson Canyon is a significant, submarine canyon that begins from the shallow outlet of New York Harbor (the Hudson River's mouth) and extends out over 450 miles seaward across the continental shelf. Then the canyon finally connects to the deep ocean basin at a depth of three to four kilometers below sea level. Next it carves through a deep notch of about one-kilometer deep in the shelf break and runs down the continental rise.

The Hudson Canyon is positioned about a hundred miles east of the Hudson River's mouth off the New Jersey coast. Its walls rise three-quarters of a mile from its floor making it comparable to the Grand Canyon (its cliffs are over a mile deep and 270 miles long). The Hudson Canyon is the biggest known canyon off the East Coast of the United States, and one of the largest canyons in the world. Over a fifty-mile distance, the average slope of the canyon floor is 1.5 degrees. At this point the canyon is as much as seven and a half miles wide from east rim to west rim and as much as 3,609 feet deep from its rim to its floor across the continental slope.

The canyon was created during the last Ice Age, over 10,000 years ago, when the sea level was about four hundred feet lower and the mouth of the Hudson River was close to the edge of the continental shelf, approximately 100 miles east of its present site. The Hudson River discharged sediment, which helped carve the canyon aided by underwater avalanches of sand and mud. Tidal currents sweep up and down the channel; and sometimes, during severe storms, cold ocean water is pushed up the Hudson Canyon to spread out on the shelf. Thus the canyon continues to be cut by traveling sediments. Finally, in regards to navigating on the river, Hudson Canyon's location is marked by a navigational buoy that marks the seaward end of vessel traffic separation of the Hudson Canyon-Ambrose lanes to New York Harbor for Atlantic shipping.

Another important part of the Hudson estuary is that 79 tributaries (small rivers that join bigger rivers) join it at different portions of its course. These tributaries are a vital part of the river as they provide about twenty percent of the water to the Hudson, a large amount of sedimentary and carbon material, and are important habitats for a wide variety of invertebrates and fish. In fact, today interest in the Hudson River's tributaries has heightened because urbanization has affected the river's water quality and there is some scientific evidence that the most urbanized tributaries contain greatly reduced fish populations.

When it comes to knowing what the Hudson River is all about, the Upper Hudson Valley is the crucial region to our understanding of the river, since it is the location of the headwaters, contains the major tributaries into the Hudson and is at the head of the river's estuary. The Upper Hudson's major tributaries are the Hoosic and Mohawk rivers. Together the rivers supply the majority of sediments for the entire Hudson River, unique ecological areas with trout streams near the Hudson's headwaters, and exotic species in the Hudson and Mohawk Rivers.

The 70-mile long Hoosic River, also known as the Hoosac, has a stony bottom that is usually exposed and is the only river that ties together Massachusetts, Vermont, and New York. Its main stream, the south branch, rises in northwestern Massachusetts in the Hoosac Range. It flows north, west and northwest, past the Massachusetts towns of Adams, North Adams and Williamstown, and then across Pownal in the southwest corner of Vermont, before entering New York. It then continues to run past Hoosick Falls, where it provides hydroelectric power and meets the Hudson fourteen miles above the city of Troy in the town of Schaghticoke in Rensselaer County, New York.

The other major tributary of the Hudson is the Mohawk River. The eastward flowing Mohawk is both the largest and longest tributary of the Hudson River and is a major waterway in north central New York. The river flows about 143 miles east/southeast from Oneida County, entering the Hudson near Albany. The cities of Schenectady, Amsterdam, Utica and Rome are built on its banks. The river and its supporting canal, the Erie Canal, connect the Hudson River and port of New York with the Great Lakes at Buffalo, New York.

For many decades, the Mohawk River has been the crucial transportation and migration link to the west as a passage between New York's Allegheny and Adirondack Highlands. The middle course of the Mohawk River runs through Montgomery County, where most of the village sites of the Mohawk Nation of the Iroquois Confederacy are located. The Mohawks left the region during the American Revolution.

Other main Hudson tributaries include the Croton River, Esopus Creek, Rondout Creek, Annsville Creek and the Saw Kill River.

The Croton River is a river in southern New York that begins where the East and West branches of the Croton River meet a little ways downstream from the Croton Falls Reservoir. Shortly downstream, the Croton River flows into the Muscoot Reservoir and after flowing through that, it empties into the New Croton

Reservoir. Then shortly after that, the water leaves the spillway at the New Croton Dam and finally empties into the Hudson River at Croton-on-Hudson, New York.

Esopus Creek, another Hudson tributary, is a small river in southeastern, New York. The Esopus Creek joins the Hudson by the village of Saugerties in the northeast corner of Ulster County.

The Esopus originates at Winnisook Lake in the Catskill Mountains, and flows in a circle around Panther Mountain. It then eventually continues eastward until it runs north into the Hudson at Saugerties. The creek is also a component of New York City's water supply system.

Another creek, which is a tributary of the Hudson, is Rondout Creek located in Ulster County, NY. Rondout rises on Rocky Mountain in the eastern Catskills, rolls south to New York City's Rondout Reservoir, then into the valley between the Catskills and the Shawangunk Ridge.

Most of the land surrounding the creek is part of New York's Forest Preserve and is undeveloped. This rocky waterway boasts several popular swimming holes, one of, which is known as Blue Hole for the greenish tone of the deep water within. Eventually, toward the end of its course, the Rondout Creek goes over the beautiful High Falls, turns north, then east again, before finally reaching the Hudson along the south border of Kingston, NY.

Another Hudson River tributary is Annsville Creek that flows south out of the Highlands into Peekskill Bay, NY. The creek and mudflats are substantially cut off from Peekskill Bay and the Hudson by railroad property. The creek has a medium-sized area of brackish intertidal mudflats.

In addition to Annsville Creek, there's the Saw Kill River that represents two different bodies of water in New York. Both of these bodies are tributaries of the Hudson River, on its east bank. One empties into Tivoli Bay, near Red Hook and the other one, about 30 miles north, empties into the Hudson at Stuyvesant Landing, New York.

And since it's a large river, the Hudson River has yet even more tributaries. Some of them include the Saw Mill River, Battenkill, Fishkill Creek, and the North River.

The Saw Mill River is a 20-mile long tributary that flows from Chappaqua to Yonkers (in Westchester County), where it empties into the Hudson. Battenkill is a 50-mile river arising in Vermont, which runs into New York and is known for its fishing. Fishkill Creek, another tributary, has a watershed that encompasses parts of Dutchess and Putnam counties in New York State.

Finally, there's the North River that represents the southernmost portion of the Hudson River between the states of New Jersey and New York. Regarding commercial vessel usage, the North River is the part of the river from the Hudson River's mouth to about the bend where the Hudson turns from south-southwest to south at about 30th Street in Manhattan, and close to the northern boundary of Hoboken, New Jersey.

Piers along the Hudson shoreline of Manhattan were known as North River piers. In fact, North River Pier 81 is used by the Circle Line at West 41st Street and North River Pier 94 of the New York Cruise Terminal is at West 54th Street. Moreover, Hagstrom Company maps, typically considered the standard in the New York metropolitan area, formerly designated the lower part of the Hudson as North River and above that as Hudson River.

Yet besides tributaries that the Hudson provides, the river is also a working waterway for commerce. Each day, river pilots navigate cargo vessels (gigantic ships, which include tankers) from all over the world on the Hudson up to Port Albany and down to the Port of New York. The river has been and continues to be one of New York State's premier natural assets and is an engine of the state's economy, sustaining multi-million dollar coastal fisheries, providing for high value residential and commercial development and providing a crucial transportation link in New York's import and export economy.

The Hudson River serves as a major commercial transportation artery for the port cities of Albany, Newburgh, Kingston and Poughkeepsie. It is where huge businesses like General Motors, IBM and General Electric chose to put down their roots. Tourism and agriculture continue to be the mainstays of the region's economy. Recreational boating has boosted the economy as well, providing revenue in sales and tourism. As for agriculture, there are about one million acres of farmland within the Hudson

River Valley, representing diverse diaries, orchards, vineyards and horticultural crops.

In addition, along the Hudson in the city of Kingston, New York, you can find the Delaware Forest, home to over 200 acres of remnant, secondary, old growth woodlands. The forest, east of Kingston, is on a limestone ridge overlooking the river, just north of the mouth of the Roundout River. This woodland is the biggest, last contiguous forest left in Kingston.

Walk into the Delaware Forest and you will see a diverse group of plants and trees such as red, white and black oak trees, white pine trees and hemlock trees. Visitors can also catch scenic views of the Hudson riverscape from the east and south edges of the ridge. From the ridge's northwest edge, you can see the high peaks of the Catskill Mountains.

Besides the terrain, which surrounds the river, the Hudson is one of the most biologically productive rivers on the East Coast of the U.S. Submerged habitat in the Hudson is composed of partially exposed and exposed wetland plant communities. The habitat types of plants include the river's bottom and submerged aquatic vegetation (SAV). Between Westchester and Rockland counties, the riverbed of the Hudson River consists of layers of silt hundreds of feet deep with bedrock over 300 feet below sea level.

Beds of submerged aquatic vegetation are subtidal plant communities, which occur in water as much as 6 feet below low tide. The ecological functions of these aquatic beds are diverse. SAV in the Hudson River include native plants such as water celery and clasping-leaved pondweed as well as nonnative species like Eurasian water milfoil and curly pondweed. The plants act as nurseries for a variety of fish species and produce organic matter, which is an integral part of the river's food web. Submerged aquatic vegetation beds also enhance the clarity of the Hudson. These plants also take in nutrients through their leaves and roots, decreasing the likelihood of alga blooms. During calm periods in the river, they can filter suspended sediments leading to better water clarity.

In addition, SAV beds in the Hudson provide important habitat and feeding areas for waterfowl such as ducks. And wading birds like the great blue heron and the snowy egret often feed on submerged aquatic vegetation at low tide.

The Hudson River Estuary (a water passage where the tide meets a river current) is a provider of critical nursery and spawning grounds for a wide variety of fish species and is part of the great Atlantic flyway for migratory birds. The river's tidal flats and marshes give essential nutrients to the first links in a food web that extends throughout the river and far into the Atlantic Ocean.

Yet way above the Hudson River's tides in northern New York State are two famous, majestic and scenic mountains, the Adirondacks and Catskills, both covering and towering over the eastern part of the state. The gigantic Adirondack Mountains represent New York's main landform and is a heavily forested area. The Catskills, south of the Adirondacks (about 33 miles from Albany, NY), has a sublime appearance and stands at the western bank of the river. Both the Adirondacks (as I stated earlier, its highest point is at 5,344 feet) and the Catskills (highest mountain has an elevation of 4,180 feet) can be seen for miles along the Hudson. Moreover, these two historic, mighty mountains provide and support a variety of life forms throughout the Hudson Valley's ecosystem.

In addition to the upper Hudson's nearby mountainous terrain, the river flows through the area's geological lineations as it slices across a series of rugged terranes. The mid-Hudson cuts through early and middle-Paleozoic sedimentary rocks, with the Catskill Mountains to the west and the Taconic Mountains to the east. And although the Hudson River was above the Taconic Mountains millions of years ago, it still was able to erode down fast enough to maintain its original path. Thus the Hudson cuts through the Taconic Mountains between Newburgh and Peekskill, NY instead of finding an easier route elsewhere.

In fact, the geologic history of the Delaware Water Gap (Delaware River on the New Jersey/Pennsylvania Border) is similar to that of the Hudson River. At the Delaware Water Gap, surface layers of rock were folded into long ridges instead of fracturing into the Taconic Mountains. Like the Hudson River, a long period of erosion followed the original mountain building that resulted in a nearly flat surface. The Delaware River then developed southeastward across this flat surface. As for the Hudson River, after it slices through the Taconic Mountain range, it then rolls through the Hudson Highlands where early Paleozoic geological formations trend directly east to west across the river's flow path in the area of West Point.

Beneath the mid-Hudson region, the Hudson flows past the Triassic volcanic cliffs of the Palisades in New Jersey and then runs past the New York group, which is a series of early Paleozoic metamorphic and Proterozoic rocks and then it moves past a series of terminal deposits of the last glacial epoch. Along the whole stretch of the lower Hudson, the steep banks and cliffs along its shoreline impress many people. Most other estuaries in America just meander to the sea along a broad low-relief flood plain.

As I just mentioned, geology of the river is indeed significant to its beauty, its past and uniqueness. Rocks along both sides of the river, throughout its valley and adjacent mountains record a complex and long geologic history. For instance, the Hudson Highlands, which run north to Breakneck and Storm King Mountains, consist of more than 1 billion-year-old, coarsely crystalline granites and beautiful marble-cake gneisses. These rocks represent the bedrock of the region and the heart of our continent. Over the years, metamorphic rocks have suffered intense pressures and temperatures from overlying rocks. And although they are unfractured and hard, it's incredible that the deepest part of the Hudson River cuts through them.

Besides geology, with the Hudson River's historic mansions, castles and century-old lighthouses, it reflects a more romantic era. The river also flows near thousands of acres of parkland, sandy beaches, rolling hills, highland plains and steep cliffs. Boating, fishing, swimming and hiking are just some of the many things you can see and enjoy on its water and shores. Besides historic attractions and recreational points of interest, the river has also been a breeding ground for politics. Hundreds of advocacy groups have formed around the Hudson River debating over environmental dredging pits. The breathtaking scenery of the Hudson Valley has also intrigued filmmakers. For instance, filmmaker Peter Hutton made a film of the Hudson titled "Study of a River" in 1997. That particular film brings the viewer back to the physical presence of the Hudson River in relation to the Holland Tunnel Ventilation Building. Overall, the Hudson River is a beautiful, beloved, dynamic and ever-changing river. It is a resource to protect for us and for future generations.

Chapter 1
Aquatic Plants, Habitats, Hudson River Estuaries (tributaries within the estuaries), Its Ecosystem, Fish & Wildlife

Ecosystems are made up of multiple habitats. Residents are familiar with the mosaic of old fields, wetlands and woodlands that spread across the Hudson Valley. Some species, like the bobcat, need huge tracts of unbroken forests, while bluebirds prefer open fields. Blanding's turtles need a specific mix of ponds and uplands to complete their life cycle.

Beneath the surface of the Hudson River is an unseen mosaic of habitats as diverse as that on land. Hudson River habitat includes patches of underwater plants, reaches of submerged bedrock and fringing wetlands.

The patches of underwater plants, also called submerged aquatic vegetation (SAV), serve important ecological functions. These plants keep the water column filled with oxygen needed by fish and other aquatic creatures to breathe, protect small fish from predators and provide a habitat for aquatic insects central to the aquatic food chain. These plant beds are an incubator for life underwater and many river species depend on them.

For about a decade, a group effort has been made under way to map the patches, understand their central role in the Hudson River ecosystem and monitor how the beds change over time. In general, these areas are performing well, with abundant and distinct numbers often twice as high as in bare patches. Yet despite the huge areas covered by these plant beds in the Hudson and their importance to the ecosystem functioning, there are reasons why people must monitor changes in the condition or extent of the river's ecosystem.

All aquatic plants are not alike. Casual sightseers and boaters of the Hudson are probably familiar with water chestnut, a floating exotic plant with barbed seeds (also called "devil heads"). Its thick mats can be a challenge for boaters trying to navigate through shallow waters. Scientists, ecologists, environmentalists and researchers believe that many of the areas presently occupied by water chestnut used to contain a diversity of truly submerged plants.

Other plants found under the Hudson include water-celery, a native plant that is valued as a food source for waterfowl, such as the canvasback duck. Water-celery plant beds occur in shallow portions of the river where water is less than nine feet deep. Beds can be as big as 25 acres, although most are much smaller. In some reaches of the Hudson, as much as 25 percent of the river bottom is covered with these plants. In the stretch of the river around Dutchess and Ulster counties, one-quarter to one-half of the shoreline is ringed with plant beds. The largest in the Hudson is in the center of the river directly under the Kingston-Rhinecliff Bridge.

Sprouting from over-wintering buds in June, water-celery is only seen during low tides in July and August. From above water at mid and high tides, it is difficult to detect these submerged plants because they are almost invisible. Near invisibility puts these plants at risk and they are easily damaged by motorboat passage and anchoring. Water-celery plants also play an important role in maintaining dissolved oxygen levels in the Hudson River for aquatic animals. For example, in large beds of celery, dissolved oxygen concentrations can persist for four to six hours per day. On sunny days, you can actually see bubbles on the plant's blades.

There is also a large community of aquatic animals associated with river plant beds like dragonfly nymphs and small crustaceans. These species may not occur in other parts of the river and are totally dependent on vegetated patches.

Some small fish, including the spot-tail shiner and young white perch, use plant beds and algae as refuge from predators, shelter from currents and a food source. And even though submerged aquatic vegetation in the Hudson is often invisible, it plays an important role in the health of the river. To minimize damage, management agencies and the boating public need to be aware of these underwater plants. Moreover, construction permits along the shoreline should not be issued without considering the possible impact on aquatic vegetation.

Aquatic vegetation must have a suitable habitat to grow in the river. One area in particular is the lower Hudson River Estuary. The lower Hudson River Estuary is the portion of the Hudson River extending from the Battery at the southern tip of Manhattan north to Stony Point at the northern end of New York's Haverstraw

Bay. This estuary is used as a shipping channel and a little more than half of it is composed of marshes and wooded swamps. The rest is made up of mud flats that are flooded at high tide.

Towns in New Jersey located along the lower Hudson Estuary include Alpine, Edgewater, Englewood Cliffs, Fort Lee, Guttenburg, Hoboken, Jersey City, North Bergen, Tenafly, Weehawken and West New York. New York communities include The Bronx, Clarkstown, Cortlandt, Greenburgh, Haverstraw, Manhattan, Mount Pleasant, Nyack, Orangetown, Ossining, Peekskill, Stony Point and Yonkers.

The physical conditions in the lower Hudson River are controlled by freshwater flow in the river, tidal variations at the downstream ocean end, and the surface mass depending on the meteorological conditions in the region. The lower Hudson Estuary includes all riverine and estuarine habitats, including open water and tidal wetlands in this particular stretch of the river. This section of the Hudson is the major site of river water mixing with ocean water in the Hudson Estuary and includes the moderate and high salinity zones of the river. This estuary area is a regionally significant nursery and wintering habitat for a number of estuarine, anadromous and marine fish species. It is also a migratory and feeding area for fish and birds that feed on the abundant fish and benthic invertebrate resources in this area.

Along the lower Hudson Estuary, its uplands and shoreline are in a mosaic of private and public ownership. New York City owns a huge portion of Manhattan's West Side while much of the western shoreline of the Hudson from Fort Lee, New Jersey, north to Haverstraw, New York, is part of the Palisades Interstate Park system. Underwater lands are also under public ownership; for instance, New York City holds grants to most underwater lands to the pierhead limit. As for the state, the New York State Department of State has designated many Significant Coastal Fish and Wildlife Habitats within this stretch of the Hudson; these include Lower Hudson Reach, Piermont Marsh, Croton River and Bay, and Haverstraw Bay.

The Hudson River can be divided into salinity habitat zones based on average annual salinities: the polyhaline (high salinity) zone from Manhattan north to Yonkers; the mesohaline (moderate salinity) zone from Yonkers to Stony Point; the oligohaline zone from Stony Point north to about Wappingers Falls; and the tidal freshwater zone from Wappingers Falls north to the Troy Dam. These salinity zones differ greatly within the season, with the salt front pushed as far back as the Tappan Zee Bridge or upper harbor during high spring flows and brackish water extending as far north as Poughkeepsie during low summer flows. The Hudson River is partially regulated by the Hudson River-Black River Regulating District, one goal of which is to minimize spring flooding in the upper Hudson (above the Troy Dam) and to provide some augmentation flows during the low flow periods. A secondary goal is providing freshwater flows during drought conditions to assist in keeping the salt front below the freshwater intakes at Poughkeepsie.

The lower Hudson River estuary zone from Manhattan to Stony Point is an area that approaches marine habitat characteristics, having very strong semi-diurnal (twice daily) tidal currents and moderate salinities generally in the range of 5 to 30 parts per thousand, but with lower salinities during spring runoff. This section of the Hudson is typically the zone of greatest mixing of river water and ocean water. The salt front where the ocean water and lower salinity river water meet also functions as a nutrient and plankton trap, making this zone of the river the most productive in terms of zooplankton and phytoplankton. During periods of high freshwater flow, much of the plankton is flushed out of the river; the exception is the shallow bays that trap some of the plankton. In addition, plankton is carried into the lower estuary with ocean waters on flood tide. High turbidity in this part of the estuary may limit primary productivity, with a range of sunlight penetration from one to five meters below the river's surface.

In Manhattan, along the Hudson, is where you'll find the Hudson River Park Estuarine Sanctuary, the park's water area consists of about 400 acres and the sanctuary's habitat is a major channel shoreline within the lower Hudson River Estuary.

About 70 species of fish have been reported in this area, where most of the species that are commonly seen are cunner, weakfish, winter flounder, Atlantic menhaden, Atlantic silverside, white perch, spotted hake, hogchoker, bay anchovy and seaboard goby. Anadromous species (fish that swim from the ocean to the river for breeding) that are commonly found in the Estuarine

Sanctuary during the spring and fall include American shad, alewife and Atlantic tomcod. The only catadromous species (fish that move from the river to the ocean for breeding) found in the sanctuary is the American eel. Eels spawn at sea and their young move to the Hudson Estuary during the spring.

Birds also utilize different habitats along the Hudson River Park Estuarine Sanctuary's shoreline during the spring for feeding, nesting and overwintering. In the fall, the birds use this area for migration. In fact, many waterfowl species mainly black duck, mallards, Canadian geese and gadwall, breed in and around the New York Harbor. In addition, American black ducks, canvasback ducks and over 30 species of shorebirds regularly migrate through the park for food. Osprey, Peregrine Falcon and the common barn owl breed in the Hudson River Park Estuarine. Birds that commonly overwinter in this area include the rough-legged hawk, the short-eared owl and the long-eared owl. Songbirds migrate and overwinter in and around the Port of New York and breeding songbirds consist of the gray catbird, red-winged blackbird, yellow warbler, song sparrow and American robin.

The New York Harbor area indeed lies within a section of the Hudson's lower estuary. However, there are two distinct sections of the river within the lower estuary. The first, from the Battery to the New York-New Jersey State line, is narrow, with an average width of about 5,000 feet, an average depth of about 40 feet and semi-diurnal tides of 4 to 5 feet. There is only a narrow band of shallow subtidal flats along the shore. Most of the shoreline habitat, especially from Manhattan north to Croton-on-Hudson, is disturbed from industrial, commercial and residential development that has filled substantial areas. An exception is the small natural shoreline and wetland complex at the mouth of the Spuyten Duyvil (Harlem River) at New York City's Inwood Hill Park. Extensive pier, inter-pier and pile field areas dominate the shoreline in the lower 6 miles of the Hudson River. Above Fort Lee, New Jersey, the western shoreline is bombarded by a rocky talus slope shoreline at the base of the Palisades.

The second section of the river lies on the northern part of the lower estuary from the New York State line north to Stony Point, consists of the Tappan Zee, the Haverstraw and Croton Bays and is known as the wide bays region. In this region, the river is much wider (3.5 miles wide) and shallower (6 to 12 feet deep), except for the 40-foot deep channel. In Haverstraw Bay, the channel is maintained by dredging at the depth of 32 feet.

In regards to tributaries at the lower part of the river, the lower Hudson Estuary has only a few minor freshwater tributaries such as the Sawmill River, Sparkill Creek, Cedar Pond Brook, Minisceongo Creek and Furnace Brook. The only major tributary in this zone is the Croton River and its flow has been reduced by impoundments for New York City's Croton Reservoir system. With the exception of Piermont marshes, Grassy Point marshes, and the mouth of the Croton River, there is a notable absence of marshes in this stretch of the river. The shorelines of the Wide Bays Region support less intense development, a mixture of industrial and commercial uses, than does the lower section. As for marshes in the river, Piermont Marsh is a 1,000-acre brackish wetland complex that includes a large, brackish tidal marsh and adjacent intertidal mudflat grading into a shallow subtidal aquatic bed. The brackish tidal marsh is dominated by common reed and narrow-leaved cattail with some salt marsh species including spike grass, rose mallow and saltmeadow cordgrass. Whereas the shallow water in Haverstraw Bay supports huge areas of submerged aquatic vegetation while Croton Bay has extensive aquatic vegetation beds.

The lower Hudson supports local fish populations as well as populations of migratory and wintering birds that feed on the rich fish and benthic resources. There are 240 species of special emphasis regularly using the lower Hudson River Estuary, incorporating 151 bird species and 80 fish species. In the lower Hudson River Estuary, primary production is moderate and zooplankton populations are extremely variable; both marine and estuarine forms occur. Copepods dominate the zooplankton community in that it decreases with increased distance from the New York-New Jersey Harbor. Meroplanktons (organisms that spend only part of their life cycle as plankton), invertebrate larvae, and fish larvae, dominate the lower river in the summer. In the estuary, meroplankton can range from 1,000 to 400,000 individuals per cubic meter, whereas copepod abundance can range from 1 to 90 individuals per cubic meter in the estuary. Shellfish species are plentiful, including soft clam, northern quahog and eastern oyster;

however, the waters are not certified for human consumption of these shellfish. The river's predominant crustaceans consist of sand shrimp, grass shrimp and blue crab. The early life stage of blue crab larvae need high salinities and therefore, the lower Hudson Estuary is a prime adult blue crab spawning region.

The lower Hudson Estuary is also utilized by a vast number of marine spawners as a nursery area because it provides a great habitat for the early crucial life cycles of fish and invertebrate species (mentioned in the previous paragraph). The lower Hudson River Estuary ranks among the most productive systems on the northern Atlantic coast for fisheries. Marine finfish that are found in this area include fourbeard rockling, American eel, Atlantic menhaden, bluefish, weakfish, longhorn sculpin, and northern pipefish. Estuarine fish that spawn in this section of the Hudson include hogchoker, winter flounder, bay anchovy, and mummichog.

The lower reach of the Hudson River is an important wintering habitat for young-of-the-year, yearling and older striped bass between mid-November and mid-April. These fish spawn upriver to Haverstraw Bay and use nursery areas in Haverstraw Bay and the Tappan Zee before moving downriver to overwinter, typically feeding on the huge number of invertebrates living in this area. A large number of yearling winter flounder also occupy this part of the river during the winter. There are 23 fish species dominated by five species in the Upper Bay of New York Harbor/Hudson River Estuary region. The five dominant fish species, which were most abundant during the spring and summer in that area, include American shad, bay anchovy, winter flounder, Atlantic tomcod and alewife.

In the New Jersey part of the lower Hudson River to the Piedmont Province, 40 fish species and 20 invertebrates were discovered. The majority of species found throughout that area were bay anchovy, blueback herring, alewife, hogchoker, white perch, American eel, Atlantic tomcod, American shad, winter flounder and striped bass. Moreover, the area in New Jersey between Edgewater and Jersey City was found to be an important habitat for striped bass. Besides fish, this lower Hudson area has mass concentrations of wintering waterfowl, especially canvasback. Other birds found there are mergansers, scaup, mallard and Canadian geese. In addition, bald eagles now overwinter along the lower Hudson reach (habitat on the west side of the Hudson in New Jersey), with a roost site in the Palisades.

The Palisades is a narrow ridge situated on the western shoreline of the Hudson River in northeastern New Jersey and southeastern New York, at the northern end of the New York City region. The eastern boundary of the Palisades habitat complex follows the west shore of the Hudson River from just south of the George Washington Bridge in Fort Lee, NJ, north about 22 miles to Haverstraw, NY, and then west for another four miles. The western (inland) boundary of the complex parallels the river boundary; the two encompass the open space on the Palisades Ridge. The Palisades consists of regionally unique talus slope and traprock communities and is important open space within the urban core by the Hudson for resident and migratory songbirds and raptors.

Palisades is part of the Northern Triassic Lowlands (Newark Basin) of the Piedmont province. The Palisades creates the eastern edge of a sill made up of intrusive lava known as traprock that was intruded during the Triassic period (about 200 million years ago). This traprock is more resistant to erosion than are surrounding sandstones that have been worn down to lower elevations. The resulting ridges, with elevations over 600 feet, stand out tremendously above the Hudson River. Also cliffs, ridges, and talus slope communities support many regionally unique species and communities.

The top of the Palisades Ridge is mainly forested and is basically a mixed-oak forest community dominated by red oak, black oak, white oak, sugar maple, black birch, tulip tree and different vines such as wild grape, moonseed, catbrier and poison ivy. Other nearby wooded areas includes a hemlock-hardwood forest inundated with red maple and eastern hemlock. There are also dry areas that grow red cedar, red oak, hickory and chestnut oak trees.

The talus slopes that occur at the bottom of the cliffs along the Palisades consist of huge barren traprock boulders with little or no soil. Water, ice and snow trapped beneath the boulders make microhabitats with temperatures ranging from ten to fifteen degrees Fahrenheit. Dominant trees and shrubs in this area include black birch, paper birch, Eastern hemlock, white pine, sassafras, Virginia creeper and American basswood.

The Palisades area along the Hudson is special and important because it represents some of the only remaining space in the greater New York City area. The Palisades is also home to an array of wildlife. In fact, for many years, the Peregrine Falcon has nested on the Palisades Cliffs. In 1995, bald eagles were seen overwintering at the Palisades. That was the first year since the 1950s that eagles were regularly spotted here.

As for the northern end of the Palisades Ridge, it curves west and abuts the Hudson Highlands. The open space at the southern section of the Palisades connects the Hackensack Meadowlands through open space corridors along the upper Hackensack River and Overpeck Creek.

On the ridge, the forest communities support migratory and breeding areas for a variety of birds, including songbirds such as the ovenbird and wood thrush. Regionally rare birds nesting in the Palisades consist of the Cooper's hawk and the redheaded woodpecker. More than 230 birds have been identified at Greenbrook Sanctuary (northern New Jersey part of the Palisades) and normally over eighty species of birds can be seen in one day during migration. Moreover, the relatively unfragmented forest habitats on the Palisades also support populations of two turtle species, the eastern box turtle and the wood turtle.

Yet despite the wildlife that lives at the Palisades, that area faces special problems that need to be addressed by environmentalists and wildlife officials. For example, the Allegheny woodrat population is now threatened due probably by parasitic roundworms spread by raccoons. In addition, rare traprock communities will be degraded by human disturbance. Finally, development of land around the parks in the Palisades is fragmenting the forest and that may result in the loss of rare plants and communities.

Suggested solutions to the above problems are that active protection of the Allegheny woodrat may be needed, including trapping and removing raccoons, inoculating rats against roundworm and reintroducing them to occupied habitats. Also more restoration efforts are needed for Peregrine Falcons to return to their old nesting sites in the Palisades and protection of these sites may be appropriate. In addition, a roosting habitat for wintering bald eagles should be maintained along the Hudson River and protection of the talus slope and traprock communities should be continued.

Besides the Palisades habitat on the west side of the Hudson, there's Piermont Marsh, a large intertidal brackish marsh community and one of the biggest undeveloped wetland complexes on the Hudson River. Located next to the Palisades, it comprises the northernmost occurrence of salt marsh species on the Hudson. And because Piermont symbolizes an exemplary ecological type of community, the Marsh has been designated as one of four sites that make up the Hudson River National Estuarine Research Reserve. Breeding birds, which utilize the marsh, are red-winged blackbird, marsh wren, swamp sparrow and Virginia rail. Other birds that breed there include gadwall, wood duck, black duck, pied-billed grebe, green-backed heron, American woodcock, American bittern, least bittern, king rail, sedge wren and fish crow. Moreover, huge concentrations of herons, shorebirds and waterfowl use shallows and tidal flats as staging areas for spring and fall migrations. Meanwhile, during the spring migration period, small numbers of osprey congregate in the marsh. In the shallow and marsh areas, scientists have found a great number of mummichog, killifish, fiddler crabs and blue crabs. Other wildlife species residing in Piermont Marsh include northern water snake, snapping turtle, muskrat, raccoon and mink. Rare plants include cylindrical-headed bulrush, buttonbush dodder and necklace sedge.

The eastern bank of the Hudson River is where Croton River and Croton Bay are located. This river and bay lie between the towns of Ossining and Cortlandt, New York. The tidal portions of the Croton Bay and Croton River create one of the largest sheltered shallow and mudflat areas in the main stem of the river. This bay and river area still contains a remnant submerged aquatic vegetation habitat. The Croton River also drains about 375 square miles and has an annual discharge rate of 500 cubic feet per second. All year-round, the river and bay are productive for a number of anadromous and freshwater fish. These fish are important prey to the state-listed threatened osprey, especially during migration periods. Travel between Piermont Marsh and Stony Point and you'll find the Tappan Zee and Haverstraw Bay area. This wide, shallow section of the Hudson is the area of the annual, seasonal salt front. This is the region where the freshwater from the upper river mix with the marine water of the Atlantic, make brackish water habitats. Primary (submerged aquatic phytoplankton and vegetation) and secondary (invertebrates, zooplankton and fish) biological productivity is very strong and high in this shallow water habitat. This area also serves as a main nursery and feeding area for estuarine-dependent and anadromous species. This particular section of the river is a major nursery area for tomcod, white perch, striped bass, and Atlantic sturgeon (that spawn elsewhere in the Hudson); it's also used as a wintering area for the shortnose sturgeon. The Haverstraw Bay is a crucial habitat for the estuarine-dependent fish that the Hudson River system contributes to the New York Bight. Many wintering waterfowl also use this area during spring and fall migration periods for feeding and resting. Some numbers of wintering waterfowl found in this area are scaup, common goldeneye, canvasback, mergansers, mallard, American black duck and Canada goose. Since 1985, Peregrine Falcons have used a nesting box on the Tappan Zee Bridge but have had low fledging success. A network of marshes behind Grassy Point next to Haverstraw Bay is one of the few large marshes along the lower Hudson River; however, tidal circulation has been significantly reduced by road construction and the marsh has been impacted by sewage treatment plants and landfills.

In addition to the lower Hudson River Estuary, there's the Mid-Hudson River Estuary. The significant habitat boundary for the Mid-Hudson River estuary follows the shores of the Hudson River from the wide bays region at Stony Point north to Poughkeepsie. This habitat includes the seasonal inland extent of brackish water (part freshwater, part saltwater) in the Hudson, although the limits of the zone change with the amount of freshwater flow. New York towns that sit along the Mid-Hudson River Estuary include Cornwall, Cortlandt, Fishkill, Highland, Lloyd, Marlborough, New Windsor, Newburgh, Phillipstown, Poughkeepsie, Stony Point and Wappinger.

The habitat complex boundary of the mid-Hudson Estuary consists of all estuarine and riverine open water and tidal wetland habitat (includes freshwater & salt marshes). This area represents an important spawning migratory and nursery habitat for estuarine, anadromous and freshwater fish, a significant winter-feeding and roosting areas for the bald eagle and its home to unique regional and global brackish and freshwater tidal communities and plants. Just like the lower estuary, the mid-estuary is under both private and public ownership. The bulk of the shoreline where the Hudson flows through the New York-New Jersey Highlands area (Harriman State Park, Bear Mountain State Park, Hudson Highlands State Park, Storm King State Park, West Point Military Academy and Camp Smith Military Reservation) is under public ownership. The remaining shoreline is predominately in the hands of private owners and underwater lands are owned by New York State through the Office of General Services. Wetlands are regulated in New York under the state's Freshwater Wetlands Act of 1975 and Tidal Wetlands Act of 1977; these statutes are in addition to federal regulation under Section 10 of the Rivers and Harbors Act of 1899 and Section 404 of the Clean Water Act of 1977. The state of New York has designated many Coastal Fish and Wildlife Habitats in this part of the Hudson such as Iona Marsh, Hudson River Mile 44-56, Constitution Marsh, Moodna Creek, Fishkill Creek, Wappinger Creek and Poughkeepsie Deepwater. The New York State Natural Heritage program, in conjunction with the Nature Conservancy, recognizes several high-priority sites for biodiversity with the mid-Hudson River Estuary. These sites are Poughkeepsie Deepwater Habitat (B2 - very high biodiversity significance), Con Hook (B3 - high biodiversity significance), Constitution Marsh (B3), Iona Island Marsh (B3), Mine Point (B3) and Moodna Creek Mouth (B3). Iona Island and Marsh complex has been recognized by the New York State Department of Environmental Conservation and the National Oceanic and Atmospheric Administration as part of the Hudson River National Estuarine Research Reserve. The U.S. Department of Interior has also designated Iona Island as a National Natural Landmark.

  Moving northbound on the river we will enter the Upper Hudson River Estuary. The Upper Hudson Estuary is the tidal freshwater part of the river located from Poughkeepsie north to the Federal Dam in Troy, New York. Within the Hudson River estuary, eight dams make the river navigable to barges and other huge boats. These dams make pools, which are good habitats for an array of warm water fish species. The drainage and flow pattern of the upper Hudson is complicated and consists of a number of streams passing through the early Paleozoic and Precambrian rocks of the Adirondack Mountains. By comparison, the lower Hudson takes a straight shot to its terminus.

On the river's shoreline, towns along New York State's Upper Hudson Estuary consist of Albany, Athens, Bethlehem, Brunswick, Catskill, Clermont, Coeymans, Colonie, Esopus, Greenbush, Greenport, Hyde Park, Livingston, Lloyd, New Baltimore, North Greenbush, Poughkeepsie, Red Hook, Rhinebeck, Saugerties, Schodack, Stuyvesant, and Ulster.

As for wetlands, such as tidal marshes, the largest number of them are found in the river's upper estuary. Moreover, the primary habitat complex boundary for the Upper Hudson River Estuary follows the shores of the Hudson from Poughkeepsie to the northern inland extent of the tidal Hudson River at Troy Lock and Dam. The boundary of the complex includes the tidal freshwater part of the river, including all open water, riverine, and tidal wetlands in this portion of the river. This habitat also includes the lower portion of major tributaries feeding into this part of the Hudson, up to the first impediment to fish passage in each tributary. The Upper Hudson River Estuary and its tributaries encompass a regionally important habitat for different species of fish, rare tidal freshwater wetland communities, plants and wildlife. Regarding ownership of the Upper Hudson Estuary, its shoreline and uplands are mainly under the hands of private owners. However, some underwater lands are owned by New York State under the Office of General Services (OGS). In addition, the National Park Service owns small parcels of shoreline affiliated with the Vanderbuilt and Franklin D. Roosevelt homes.

In regards to the Hudson's deepwater tidal river zones, the two sections of deepwater within the upper estuary are the northern half of Poughkeepsie Deepwater and Kingston Deepwater. The shallow subtidal zone occurs above the deepwater zone and below the mean low tide. This zone happens in shallow narrow subtidal bands along the deepwater portions of the tidal river, in extensive shallow waterbeds in the Hudson north of Kingston and in shallow bays along the river. The shallow subtidal zone frequently supports beds of submerged aquatic vegetation (SAV). These plants include water celery, waterweeds, naiads, and pondweeds. Two important exotic plant species in Hudson SAV communities are Eurasian water milfoil and water chestnut. The intertidal zone in the Upper Hudson Estuary includes freshwater intertidal shore communities along steep rocky shorelines, freshwater intertidal mudflats and freshwater tidal marsh communities along more gentle mud and sand shorelines. Freshwater intertidal shore communities are found on rocky or gravel-based shores, including areas along the rip-rap railroad embankments in the Hudson. Common species consist of smartweed, water-hemp, heartleaf plantain and southern estuarine beggar ticks. Intertidal mudflats occurring above mean low water are often sparsely vegetated and are typically dominated by Hudson arrowhead, grass-leaved arrowhead, kidney-leaf mud-plantain, wild rice and water parsnip.

Freshwater tidal marshes in the Hudson River are separated into the lower and upper marsh zones. The lower marsh experiences huge daily fluctuations in water levels and is characterized by peltate-leaved plants that include spatterdock, pickerelweed, big-leaved arrowhead and arrow arum. The upper marsh is at a higher elevation, is just partially flooded during the daily tidal cycle and consists of a marsh community. Plants normally found in the marsh community are river bulrush and narrow-leaved cattail. The northern stretch of the Hudson is also crucial for fish spawning grounds and is part of the wintering habitat for the shortnose sturgeon. This stretch also represents the northern end of the striped bass spawning area. The numerous tidal freshwater marshes and creeks in the Upper Hudson Estuary also serve as breeding, nursery, and migration corridors supporting shorebirds, waterfowl, and passerine birds. In addition, these unique tidal communities on the northern part of the Hudson consist of the freshwater tidal marsh, freshwater intertidal mudflats, freshwater tidal swamp and freshwater intertidal shore.

Tributaries of the Upper Hudson River Estuary are also important ecological waterways of the region. Some of these estuaries include the Esopus Estuary, Normans Kill, Ramshorn Marsh and Catskill Creek.

Esopus Estuary is located at the mouth of Esopus Creek and is a major tributary to the Upper Hudson River Estuary on the river's west bank in the town of Saugerties. This tidal wetland complex includes the lower Esopus Creek to the first wetland area, including intertidal mudflats, shallow water, tidal marsh and tidal swamp south and north of the creek mouth. The shallows and creek are important spawning, nursery, and feeding areas for fish such as alewife, smelt, blueback herring, white perch and black bass. The shallow water area at the mouth provides a habitat for American shad spawning and the tidal freshwater wetlands that support this area support a resting and feeding habitat for migrating osprey and waterfowl.

Another upper river tributary is Normans Kill located at the southern end of Albany, NY on the west side of the river. Normans Kill is the northernmost tributary that drains into the Upper Hudson River Estuary with a drainage area of 170 square miles. This area comprises the lower two miles of this huge freshwater creek from the mouth up to the falls. Normans Kill is a significant fish spawning and nursery habitat for blueback herring, alewife, white perch and smallmouth bass.

Besides Normans Kill, there's another Hudson tributary called Ramshorn Marsh. Ramshorn is a freshwater tidal wetland complex located just south of Catskill Creek and the village of Catskill. This complex covers about 600 acres along the Hudson's western shore and contains one of the biggest forested wetland areas in a natural condition in the Hudson Valley. Ramshorn Marsh is a system of high-quality intertidal mudflats, tidal marsh and tidal creeks. Black bass, American shad and other fish use this area as a spawning and nursery habitat and huge concentrations of migrating waterfowl use this area as a resting and feeding habitat during the spring and fall. This area also supports rare plants such as swamp lousewort, kidneyleaf mud-plantain, and estuarine beggar ticks.

Another tributary you will find on the upper stretch of the Hudson is Catskill Creek located in the town of Catskill on the western side of the river. This riverine habitat extends from the mouth of the falls just downstream of the New York State Route 23 bridge that includes Kaaterskill Creek as its first fish barrier. Fish such as white perch, alewife, blueback herring, and black bass spawn in this creek. The creek's upper end serves as a unique cold-water stream with steep-sided gorges and white water.

The entire Hudson River Estuary crosses various kinds of bedrock and its sediment transport is greatly influenced by tidal currents and strong runoff events. The small contribution of tributary input in the estuarine part of the Hudson River allows comparing the relative influence of these different factors on morphology and sedimentary processes. In fact, scientists have found that a canalized section of the Hudson shows the influence of human alteration on the morphology and possibly on related sediment transport.

The river's load of sediment derives mainly from clays eroded from surficial glacial lake and glacial outwash deposits. Otherwise, the major stem of the Hudson moves through resistant rocky terrain, which does not provide much sedimentary material. Yet because of the two-layered flow of the river in the New York Harbor area, up-current flow in the deep layer carries sediment from the ocean to within the estuary.

In any case, despite the amount of sediment and bedrock found in the river, the Hudson's estuary is subject to a tidal cycle. In fact, every 6 hours, the tides in the Hudson will shift pushing water into the river mouth on a flood tide and pulling water back out the mouth on an ebb tide. Depending upon location in the river, the vertical tide range can be less than three feet up to five feet. Just north of the Piermont Pier, extensive mud flats are exposed during low tide. The difference of elevation between high and low tides makes tidal currents. The timing of these currents mimics the rise and fall of the tides, following an approximate six-hour schedule. Excessive rainfall or strong winds can impact the currents by overwhelming them. In some portions on the river, change in watercolor can reflect the current. Due to tides and currents, the Hudson does not flow in one direction. Because the ebb tide is stronger than the flood tide, the river does eventually flush itself, but residence time in the river can differ depending upon the season and can take up to four months. During the summer, water residence time in the river increases.

In addition to tides and currents, an array of habitats and life forms exist in the lower, middle or upper estuaries of the river. For instance, faunal and vegetation communities in and along the entire Hudson River exist and depend upon depth and salinity. The deepwater tidal river zone occurs beneath the depths that support plant growth, about six feet in the turbid Hudson. Main production in this zone comes only from phytoplankton. These deepwater zones typically have swift currents and rocky bottoms. As for salinity, it influences the distribution and function of both plants and animals within the entire Hudson Estuary. Salinity zones in the Hudson River are found in the Hudson and Mohawk Rivers at Troy (Nontidal Fresh Zone), the Troy Dam to about Wappinger Falls, all Hudson tributaries to head of tide (Tidal Fresh Zone), Wappinger Falls to Stony Point (Oligohaline Zone), Stony Point to Yonkers (Mesohaline Zone), Yonkers to Manhattan (Polyhaline Zone) and the Manhattan seaward Harbor Estuary (Euhaline Zone). These salinity zones differ greatly with the season; the salt front pushes as far south as the George Washington Bridge some years during high spring flows and brackish water extends as far north as Poughkeepsie during summer low water flows. The Hudson River estuary is a tidally dominated system, with tidal flows from 10 to 100 times the freshwater inflows. Salinity influences the function and distribution of both plants and animals in the estuary. The distribution of tidal marsh communities and plants in the Hudson is influenced by surface water salinity during the growing season. Freshwater tidal marsh communities typically occur north of Newburgh-Beacon, brackish tidal marsh communities usually occur south of Newburgh-Beacon, and small salt marshes occur south of Yonkers. Benthic communities differ in distribution depending upon bottom water salinity, which is normally marine benthos from Stony Point south dominated by worms and crustaceans, a mixture of marine and freshwater organisms between Stony Point and Poughkeepsie and freshwater snails, clams and insects north of Poughkeepsie. Estuarine and coastal fish species tolerate a wide range of salinities, while freshwater species can only tolerate a narrow range to reproduce and live successfully. Anadromous fish species require various salinities at different phases of their life cycles.

In addition to depth and salinity, turbidity is another important component in the river water. Turbidity determines the muddiness or cloudiness of the water. A major source of the Hudson River's turbidity is related to the high sediment it carries, collecting and depositing mud as the water flows backward and forward along the river channel. While scientists state that a lot of sediment is not desirable, a turbid river does not equate to a dirty river that needs to be cleaned. Turbidity can reflect high levels of plankton productivity (phytoplankton & zooplankton) and huge amounts of decaying plant material that are a food source for aquatic and marine species. Murkiness in the river can benefit protecting young fish from predators. The amount of turbidity in the Hudson can vary in various parts of the river and in relation to many factors such as the amount of submerged vegetation, runoff volume and the amount of productivity.

Regarding the zones of the Hudson River, the deepwater tidal river zone occurs below the depths that support plant growth, about six feet in the turbid Hudson. Primary production in this zone comes only from phytoplankton. These deepwater zones normally have swift currents and rocky bottoms. The two-deepwater sections in the mid-estuary are Hudson River (river miles 44 to 56) and the Poughkeepsie Deepwater. The shallow subtidal zone occurs below mean low tide but above the deepwater zone. Submerged aquatic vegetation may grow in shallow, narrow, subtidal bands along the shoreline. Examples of these under river plants include waterweed (Elodea nuttallii), coontail, naiad, sago pondweed, horned pondweed and widgeon grass. Water chestnut occupies substantial portions of this part of the river from river mile 58(Pollapel Island) north to about river mile 65(Chelsea). The tidal zone in the Hudson River consists of sparsely vegetated inter-tidal flats and shore along with tidal marsh communities. Due to the generally steep shoreline, strong currents and deep water in this stretch of the Hudson, tidal flats and marshes occur only at the mouths of tributaries or in the shelter of islands where sediment can accumulate. The four main tributaries in this part of the river are from north to south: Annsville Creek, Moodna Creek, Fishkill Creek, and Wappinger Creek.

Freshwater and brackish marshes in the Hudson can typically be divided into upper and lower marsh zones. The upper marsh contains a huge marsh community consisting of mostly narrow-leaved cattail and the common reed. In the wetter areas of the upper marsh, the cattail and reed are mixed with rice-cut grass, wild rice, sweet flag and river bulrush. The lower marsh normally experiences large daily fluctuations in water levels and is characterized by peltate-leaved plants (broad leaves on long stalks arising from the plant's base), spatterdock in deeper water and arrow arum in shallower water.

In addition to the vital marsh communities occurring at the mouths, tributaries provide freshwater inflow into the Hudson system, spawning habitat for herrings, and over-wintering areas for black bass. The adjacent uplands along the mid-estuary shoreline, especially in the New York – New Jersey Highlands, support a variety of rare animal and plant species.

The Hudson River Estuary is an estuary, which supports significant populations of wildlife and fish as well as rare plants and communities. The Mid-Hudson River estuary supports a mix of freshwater, brackish and marine communities. As for the river's ecosystem, it encompasses the entire Hudson River, including its connection with the sea and its entire drainage basin. As you begin at the coast near the Battery in New York City, move up the estuary and sample the fauna, a distinct changing pattern in species richness (number of species) can be detected. The shore is dominated by fully marine species, which disappear about mid-estuary being replaced by estuarine species. These species are then replaced by fresh water species as you proceed further north.

One region of the Hudson River is the Foundry Cove, an area that is a traditional zone. During dry summers, the salinity can be up to five parts per thousand, allowing some low-salinity estuarine species to survive. In wetter years, the water is completely salt free. Most shallow waters are very productive compared to offshore oceanic waters; shallow waters near shore receive nutrients from rivers and terrestrial runoff. Although some nutrients are lost to the ocean by turbidity currents and by other means, generally, shallow waters are richer with nutrients than oceanic waters. As a result, phytoplankton growth begins earlier in spring and persists longer in shallow waters. While estuaries are extremely productive, other features also affect the composition of the biota. Heavy sedimentation and fluctuating salinity are also factors with which organisms must contend in estuaries. The number of species in estuaries is low (as compared to other high productivity brackish/marine environments), but the densities of the resident species are very high.

The Hudson River Estuary contains several distinct habitats: open water habitats dominated by phytoplankton, zooplankton, pelagic fishes, and protected water habitats (coves and marshes) along with mud flats with associated tidal creeks. Approximately 55 river miles from the Battery (location of South and Foundry Coves), where the salinity only reaches about five times of low fresh water flow, the predominant habitats near shore are marshes, coves and open water habitats in the main body of the river. The marshes in this area are typically fresh-water marshes and the upper third of the Hudson is dominated by fresh water wetlands. These habitats vary in species composition and productivity but are linked by the movement of nutrients and organisms in complex ways.

Marshes are protected shore areas where macrophytes are the main producers and stabilizers of sediment. Aquatic macrophytes are terms that normally refer to macroscopic forms of vegetation including true and macroalgae angiosperms. Emergent forms include the reed, Phragmites (dominant macrophyte at South & Foundry Coves), the cattail (Typha & Glyceria) and the cord grass (Spartina). Monodominant stands of emergent macrophytes like Typha and Phragmites are common in fresh water marshes while Spartina dominates in brackish or saline waters. Fresh water emergent macrophytes in temperate altitudes have a range of primary productivity values comparable to rainforest values.

Another significant habitat of the Hudson is found at the Palisades. The Palisades is a narrow ridge that lies along the western shoreline of the river in northeastern New Jersey and southeastern New York, at the northern end of the New York City region. The eastern boundary of the Palisades habitat complex follows the west shore of the Hudson River from just south of the George Washington Bridge in Fort Lee, New Jersey, north about 22 miles to Haverstraw, New York. The Palisades habitat supports a total of 42 species of special emphasis.

Chapter 2
Hudson Estuary Program, Its Ecosystem (including changes in it), Fish & other Wildlife (Con't)/River Pollution Problems & Solutions

The Hudson River Estuary Program is a unique regional partnership designed to protect, restore, conserve and enhance the estuary. The Hudson's diversity and productivity of natural resources sustain a wide array of present and future human benefits. It is a nursery for food and game fish, a water supply, a boater's playground, a shipping route, a landscape of inspiring beauty and more. The Estuary Program's logo is the Atlantic sturgeon, the largest fish living in the Hudson.

The Estuary Program was established in 1987 when the New York State Legislature passed Section 11-0306 of the Environmental Conservation Law. This law is known as the Hudson River Estuary Management Act which directs the Department of Environmental Conservation (DEC) to develop a management program for the Hudson River Estuarine District and its affiliated shorelines. The Estuarine District is defined as the tidal waters of the Hudson River, which include the tidal waters of its tributaries and wetlands from Federal Lock & Dam at Troy to the Verrazano Narrows.

The blueprint for implementing the Hudson River Estuary Program is called the Hudson River Estuary Action Plan, which was first released by Governor George Pataki in May 1996 and was last updated in 2002. The goals of the Action Plan are to protect and conserve ecosystem health, natural resources, clean up pollution and promote public use and enjoyment of the river. Action Plan projects have already expanded the understanding of key river species like striped bass, bald eagles, underwater grass beds, mapped tidal wetlands, upgraded boat launches and valuable open space on the shoreline.

Underwritten by New York State's Environmental Protection Fund, the Estuary Program has provided $4.55 million in grants for projects that will serve to implement Action Plan commitments through local initiatives. Regarding funding for the Action Plan, under Governor George Pataki, more than $173 million has been earmarked for the Hudson River Estuary. This includes $30 million from the New York State Environmental Protection Fund (EPF), an average of $6 million annually since 1996 for implementation of the Action Plan; $50 million of New York State Clean Water/Clean Air Bond Act (funds allocated for water quality and habitat restoration projects from New York Harbor to Troy) and $19.6 million as New York's share of a river-wide monitoring and track down of contaminant sources and pollution cleanup (funded through the New York-New Jersey Port Restoration Agreement). Furthermore, $22 million in additional New York State funds was approved from the 1996 Bond Act for open space, state and municipal park improvements and brown field cleanups and $51.7 million in other state EPF and federal funds for habitat restoration, waterfront revitalization, public access and non-point source pollution control.

The Hudson River estuary is host to a large diversity of animals and plants, each requiring specific condition to live, grow and reproduce. The Hudson estuary supports this rich living resource through its varied wetland habitats, tributary streams, an aquatic system which provides a variety of chemical and physical properties associated with the estuary's dynamic salinity gradient and the associated uplands bordering the estuary.

Water salinity is an important factor in the distribution of life in the Hudson Estuary. The natural salinity regime is important to maintaining the function of habitat and species diversity. Salinity in the river ranges from freshwater in the northern sections of the Hudson to salt water at its mouth. The degree of saltiness in any given location depends upon the amount of freshwater flowing over the Troy Dam and entering from other tributaries. During a wet spring with heavy freshwater runoff, the river may be fresh throughout most of its length. But during a summer draught, freshwater runoff falls to a fraction of spring flood conditions and ocean water is able to penetrate far into the estuary with brackish (part-salt, part fresh) water present 75 miles north at Poughkeepsie. In a typical year, the Hudson is freshwater from Troy to Newburgh Bay and increasingly salty from Newburgh Bay south through the Tappan Zee to New York Harbor.

Unlike a great number of other estuaries, the waters of the Hudson River are well mixed and turbulent. Except for the straight, narrow section of river from the Tappan Zee south, there is little stratification of freshwater flowing out over an intruding layer of salt water. Yet still, the Hudson remains largely productive, fueled by inputs of nutrients and detritus from the watershed and by planktonic primary production in the estuary.

The distribution of life in the Hudson River is changing and complex; it varies by season, life stage, year, and habitat. It is also influenced by range contractions, accidental introductions, and climatic changes. Different marine and estuarine life forms swim all the way to Troy. But in the Hyde Park to Castleton section of the river, biodiversity is high where freshwater, estuarine and occasional marine species meet and mix.

The Hudson's richness and diversity of life is related to the wide range of habitats present in its shallows, channel, intertidal fringes, and tributary streams. Shorebirds, waterfowl, birds of prey and a host of other vertebrate and invertebrate life forms depend on shelter and food found in the river's freshwater tidal marshes, mud flats and vegetated shallows. These habitats are found mostly north of Poughkeepsie whereas the mouths of tributary streams are hot locations of biological activity where resident fish overwinter in huge concentrations, migratory river herring spawn and water birds forage. The channel and other deep water areas are also critical habitats for fish and invertebrates.

Looking at the river's bottom, the food chain for many aquatic species depends on invertebrate fauna that live either in or on the bottom of the Hudson. A lot of aquatic species spawn (lay eggs) or seek refuge over certain substrate types.

Another aspect of the Estuary Plan is that it focuses on studying methods to protect and conserve the Hudson River and species that inhabit it such as fish. The Hudson is home to over 206 species of fish.

One fish in particular is New York State's American shad. These fish are from stocks in the Hudson and Delaware Rivers and are part of what is called the mid-Atlantic population. American shad are the largest of New York State's herring and their long jaw (which extends to behind their eye) and large size differentiates them from other members of the herring family.

American shad fish are born in the Hudson and migrate to the Atlantic Ocean. When they mature four to five years later, the shad return to the river in the spring to spawn. During spawning, shad arrive in huge schools, running up the rivers where they slowly adjust to the change from salt to fresh water. Although many American shad run up the Delaware River, the biggest run goes to the Hudson River Estuary. Their primary spawning range in the Hudson is from Kingston to Coxsackie. After spawning, the adults go back to the ocean. Shad eggs need clean and clear water to develop. Young fish born in the Hudson leave the estuary after their first summer.

Unfortunately, shad populations have been declining since the 1980s. Studies implemented by Department of Environmental Conservation biologists have traced the decline to overfishing on the Atlantic coast. Other studies have shown that shad were severely affected by power plants located in areas of the river where fish spawn. Young shad are drawn into power plants along with the water used for cooling purposes and are killed.

Luckily, shad do not eat when they are in the Hudson during their two-month spawning run which helps them avoid exposure to contaminants. As a result, shad is one of the few species of river fish that meets federal guidelines for human consumption.

Like the American shad, river herring spawn in the Hudson in the spring. Herring
are fished commercially mainly as bait for striped bass fishing. They are important not only for their commercial value but also in their place in the food chain as prey for striped bass and other predatory fish. Herring are plantivorous fish, feeding on zooplankton (tiny animals) floating in the water. Specialized "combs" in the fish's throat (named gill rakes) enable herring to strain the tiny plankton from the water while swimming along. Large herring eat other food including larger larvae, small insects, shrimp and even small fish.

Spawning stocks of river herring have declined in the river estuary over the last ten years. Possible causes include overfishing, predation by other fish and changes in the spawning location to the Mohawk River system. However, through the Estuary Action Plan, fishery managers are presently collecting data on age structure and mortality rates to document change, causes of change, and identify potential management responses.

Herring are unusual among other New York freshwater fish because they spend the bulk of their lives in the ocean and only return to freshwater to reproduce. Each year they return, migrating up huge rivers like the Hudson in large spawning runs. In New York State, the Hudson River is home to all members of the herring family. Freshwater portions of New York's Delaware River also receive herring runs, but only after the fish have traveled through bordering states.

Ocean-run alewife are also found in New York water. Alewife look like other small herring as their large eyes and deep body easily identifies them. Alewives have a short jaw that juts out when the mouth is closed.

Spawning occurs in early spring when large schools of alewives move into tidal waters from the ocean. The spawning runs begin slowly with only a few fish at a time migrating in. Young alewives are often hard to find as they hide in weedy beds and deep water during the day. Like the American shad, as autumn approaches they leave the estuary and migrate out to the ocean. In the state of New York, a large run of ocean-run alewives occurs in the Hudson River and its tributaries each spring.

Another popular species of fish, which I mentioned earlier, that live in the Hudson are striped bass. Striped bass is a very popular food and recreational fish and can live as long as 30 years. These bass need a water environment that is rich in oxygen. Striped bass are in the Hudson during the spring and eat smaller fish, particularly herring, as their main food.

Like shad, striped bass travel back and forth from the ocean to the Hudson River to complete their life cycle in the late spring and early summer. Their spawning range in the Hudson is from Croton Point, Westchester County to Catskill, Greene County. Unlike shad, striped bass are plentiful in the river. In fact, each year about a million striped bass (stripers) migrate into the Hudson to spawn. Unlike most fish that spend most of their adult lives in the ocean but migrate up streams and rivers to spawn, the seasonal movements of striped bass depend upon sex, age, degree of maturity, and the river where they were born. The main spawning activity for the whole East coast striper fishery is located in the Chesapeake Bay (where stripers are known as rockfish), Roanoke River Albemarle Sound watershed, the Hudson River, and to a smaller degree, the Delaware River and other rivers on the eastern coastline.

The stripers typically move up the Hudson in March and by mid-April will have reached Newburg, NY. By late April, they have reached Kingston and beyond. In May, when the river water has warmed to the mid- to upper 50s, striper spawning takes place. By mid-June, the main body of stripers has moved downstream and disperses in New York Harbor and along the coast. In addition, some stripers, mainly in small schools, stay in the river through the summer.

Today, the abundance of striped bass in the Hudson is credited to the coordinated management of populations in New York State and all along the Atlantic coast. The Estuary Program helped fund basic, ongoing studies necessary to this effort. Adult bass are netted in the spring to determine if there are plenty of the older fish that produce more eggs. Later in summer, a survey of the young bass born that year tracks the success of the spawning season.

Like shad and striped bass, Atlantic sturgeon is born in the Hudson River estuary.
Sturgeons are ancient fish that have existed since the age of the dinosaurs. The Atlantic sturgeon is the largest fish in the Hudson River. Adults typically grow from 6 to 8 feet long but have been known to grow to as much as 14 feet long. They can live for more than sixty years.

By the time sturgeon become five years old, sturgeons are classified as "adolescents" and depart for the Atlantic Ocean. Many years later, as mature adults, they return to the river to spawn. For females, this normally happens at about age twenty. Males return to the Hudson earlier, at about age fifteen.

In the past, sturgeons were plentiful in the Hudson. However, since 1996, it has been illegal to fish for Atlantic sturgeon because their populations have decreased dramatically. Offshore commercial trawlers often catch Atlantic sturgeon while netting for other fish. And even after they are returned to the water, some of the sturgeons die. Estuary Plan studies show that accidental catches may have interfered with the ability of the sturgeon population to rebuild to healthy numbers.

Shortnose sturgeon look like the Atlantic sturgeon but usually only grow to about three feet long. Shortnose sturgeons were an endangered species and have been protected since the 1970s. Due to that protection, now the Hudson River population of this sturgeon is the largest on the East Coast and appears to be increasing. Shortnose sturgeon uses the entire estuary during different stages of their life cycle and its spawning, wintering, and nursery areas all must be conserved. Shortnose sturgeons spawn in freshwater from Coxsackie to Troy and unlike the Atlantic sturgeon, they do not migrate out to the coast. The farthest they are found from the Hudson is in the Long Island Sound.

Other common species found in the Hudson are white perch and Atlantic tomcod yet limited data have been collected on white perch populations. The tomcod population has decreased over time and a possible factor to its population decline is that the Hudson River marks the southern edge of their range.

Bluefish and carp also can be found in the Hudson. Bluefish are popular marine game fish and are frequently spotted by anglers off the end of Piermont pier from mid-summer to late fall. Blues can also be seen in Croton Point where they swim alongside carp and perch. Bluefish have huge, sharp teeth and travel in schools to help catch their prey.

As for carp, these fish are not native species to New York waters. They were introduced into New York State waters from Asia in 1831. Carp start their spawning process in late spring and will spawn in weedbeds and grassy shallows. When spawning, they will thrash about wildly and even leap out of the water like salmon. A large female carp will produce over 10 million eggs and carp feed on a variety of foods including insects, plants, fish eggs, small baitfish, worms, and crustaceans. Carp grow to tremendous size in the Hudson because anglers largely ignore them. Many carp can grow over 50 pounds and are often found in freshwater shallows near or on mud.

In addition to carp, the Hudson River is home to catfish that include the Brown bullhead, Yellow bullhead and the white catfish.

The brown bullheads are medium sized fish (averaging about 8 to 14 inches in length) and can be found over muddy and gravel bottoms. Spawning takes place in May or June when the water temperature gets close to 70 degrees Fahrenheit. The whole spawning process can take up to several weeks and bullhead nests are normally found in a shaded spot near a log, but sometimes they will nest inside objects like in an automobile tire nailed to a boat dock. Brown bullheads are edible and are popular amongst anglers.

Yellow bullheads are not as common as the Brown bullhead and can be found in the Mid-Hudson River system and in the lower Hudson River tributaries. The Yellow bullhead is distinguished from the Brown bullhead by its white chin barbels, it's somewhat smaller (8 to 12 inches) and its tail is rounded rather than square. Like brown bullheads, yellow bullheads spawn in May or June and nests are often built near large stones or stumps. Like other catfish, yellow bullheads are edible but many fishermen don't catch them because of their limited range.

Like the Yellow bullhead, white catfish have a limited range and occur only in the lower Hudson River and in a few inland lakes. The white catfish looks like a bullhead but it grows larger than the bullhead and can be spotted in many areas of brackish water on the Hudson. Like the brown and yellow bullheads, white catfish spawn in the spring when the water temperature reaches 70 degrees Fahrenheit. Both females and males construct the nest, usually located on a sandbar, and guard their eggs and young. White catfish have potential for anglers like sportfish but it is recommended that people don't eat them because of high PCB (polychlorinated biphenyls) pollutant levels.

Another fish that lives in the Hudson is the black bass that lives in the river year round. There are two kinds of black bass (largemouth and smallmouth); both are popular among sport fishermen and the average size of Hudson bass is 2 pounds. However, the population of black bass has declined and scientists with the Estuary Program are trying to determine why. Black bass construct their nests in the shallow water of tributaries and spawn in the late spring. In winter, most black bass congregate in a few protected areas of the river.

Like black bass, blue crabs live in the Hudson year round where they feed on the bottom. The normal life span of a blue crab is about 18 to 26 months. Male and immature female blue crabs prefer areas of the estuary where the water is less salty. However, fertilized eggs require saltwater to survive, so males and females move south in the river close to the Atlantic Ocean to mate. As the young hatch, they migrate back upriver to less salty nursery areas.

Blue crabs grow by molting (shedding their shells). Molting occurs from spring to fall when temperatures are sixty degrees or higher. A blue crab molts an average of twenty-six times before it entirely matures.

Recreational and commercial crab harvesting usually happens during the summer months. At one year old, blue crabs measure about 5 inches across their shells and are considered market size. However, crabbers must be aware that it is illegal to catch egg-bearing, female blue crabs. Once trapped, the harvester must return the female crabs to the river immediately. Female blue crabs are normally much smaller in size than the males and if you look at the bottom of them, you will notice a triangle which makes up part of its stomach.

In addition to fish and shellfish, there are also American eel, which exist in the Hudson River. American eels spawn at sea but swim to coastal rivers to grow to adulthood.

Hudson River eels, born in the Sargasso Sea off Bermuda, migrate to New York Harbor and swim up the estuary as tiny, one-year-old, transparent "glass eels" only a few inches long. They become brown in color and change into elders as they drift into freshwater tributaries. That is where they may eventually grow to a length of up to three and a half feet. Young eels eat insects and older ones eat crustaceans and fish. About the age of ten, American eels return to the Sargasso Sea to breed and a new life cycle begins. Eels spawn only once and then die so due to their particular cycle, there is little information on their populations in the Hudson River to establish their status.

Whether you are fishing or crabbing, it is important for people to know that there are contaminants in the water throughout the Hudson River; among them are cadmium, PCBs (polychlorinated biphenyls), mercury, PAHs (polycyclic aromatic hydrocarbons), dioxins and dibenzofurans. Some of these contaminants were found in fish and blue crabs so people who eat them may also ingest these substances. Estuary program officials are tracking down contaminants in order to develop strategies for eventually ridding the Hudson of them. The Estuary Program has also funded testing for the most commonly eaten fish to determine the levels of contaminants discovered in them. However, until the problem of contaminants in the Hudson River is resolved, the public should always follow fish consumption advisories.

In addition to fish and crabs, Hudson River Valley supports a variety of birds like birds of prey, common and rare songbirds, waterfowl and shorebirds. Grassland, forest, wetland and coastal habitats within the valley are all unique and important for the species of bird they support.

The huge, unfragmented forests of the Catskill Mountains, Hudson Highlands, Rensselaer Plateau and Shawangunk Ridge support populations of forest thrushes and woodland warblers as well as many birds of prey such as the goshawk, sharp-shinned hawk, Cooper's hawk and red-shouldered hawk. One can also find rare species of Bicknell's Trush in the high-elevation, spruce-fir forest of the Catskills and the cerulean warbler have been spotted within the forests of the Hudson Highlands. The Catskill Mountains are home to more than 120 species of breeding birds while the Hudson Valley's grassland habitats support many declining or rare bird species such as savannah sparrows, northern harrier, vespers, sedge wren and meadowlark.

Wetlands and coastal areas contribute greatly to the diversity of birds found in the Hudson River region. Tidal wetlands along the estuary support American bittern, least bittern, black rail, egrets, osprey and many waterfowl species. The wooded swamps of the Harlem Valley (Columbia, Dutchess and Putnam counties) aid with breeding migrating warblers and red-shouldered hawk. The Narrows (westernmost section of Long Island Sound) contain important offshore island habitat for colonial wading bird rookeries. The three north shore bays of the surrounding Narrows area are among the most significant waterfowl wintering concentration sections in that region. Marshes affiliated with the bays are vital feeding and nesting areas for clapper rail and Green Heron while the area's sand beaches provide a nesting habitat for piping plover and least tern birds. The Arthur Kill area of the lower Hudson estuary is known for its major nesting colonies and foraging areas of ibises, herons and egrets. The area's three island colonies support different species of colonial wading birds and represent the biggest heronry complex in the state of New York.

This region also symbolizes an important location for a lot of Neotropical, migrant songbirds and nesting waterfowl.

Also in the Hudson River area is the Peregrine Falcon, once on the federal Endangered Species List, this falcon has now made a great comeback since the 1950s. Peregrine Falcons hunt other birds by diving after them and can reach speeds of 200 m.p.h. while diving. This falcon has been reestablished through captive breeding programs across the Northeast and now annually breeds at approximately 40 sites in New York State. The females are normally one-third larger than males and the females typically lay two to four eggs per year, which they incubate while the male hunts for food. The chicks hatch after about 35 days and both parents then hunt for food for their young. Chicks exit the nest four to five weeks after hatching. About one quarter of all active Peregrine Falcon nests in the state is discovered in the Hudson River area. In addition, the Department of Environmental Commission (DEC) has documented 11 of these falcon nests in the Hudson Valley, which include ledges of tall buildings in New York City along with all of the Hudson River bridges and cliffs in the Hudson Highlands. Maintenance work on bridges and buildings is scheduled around the falcon's spring nesting period.

Besides hawks and falcons, naturalists indicated sights of eagles along the Hudson, which go back to the 1880s. But by 1900, bald eagles were no longer breeding along the Hudson River although numbers of eagles continued to spend the winter months along the lower Hudson using the area for feeding.

Fortunately, now because of habitat restoration and protection efforts, eagle populations have rebounded by the Hudson. Since 1977, twenty eaglets have fledged on the Hudson estuary. In 2000, four pairs of eagles nested on the river and produced ten eaglets. And the numbers during the winter continue to increase with up to 100 eagles, which use the Hudson for winter feeding and roosting. The Hudson's neighboring river, the Delaware River, supports the largest bald eagle concentrations in New York State. Both the Hudson and Delaware Rivers are now crucial for the life cycle of eagles, which each summer, migrate across the northeast and eastern Canada.

Reptiles and amphibians are also found in the Hudson River Valley, specifically turtles, salamanders and frogs. Huge wetlands of the Hudson Valley scattered across Putnam, Dutchess, Ulster and Orange counties are home to diverse types of turtles found in New York State. Some of these turtles include bog turtle, Blanding's turtle and eastern box turtle.

The Hudson Highlands and Shawangunk ridge are also important habitat areas for wood turtles and spotted turtles. The diamondback terrapin turtle can be found in the lower Hudson estuary.

Besides turtles, many amphibians such as frogs and salamanders have been found throughout the Hudson Valley. These amphibians which made the Hudson Valley their home include: the northern cricket frog, marbled salamander, spotted salamander, blue spotted salamander, four-toed salamander, Jefferson salamander and longtail salamander.

Each year, November is the best month for hikers and sightseers to spot wildlife along the Hudson. In November, the forest floor's leaves are mostly fallen and crisp. With fewer leaves to hide them, Hudson Valley's mammals such as river otter, fisher, white-tailed deer, black bear and the occasional moose are more easily seen. In addition, beavers will diligently drag their birch cuttings into ponds, lakes and quiet stretches of the Hudson. They secure these "winter snacks" by jabbing them into the soft bottom for a time when ice will cover their homes. November is also a month of big game hunting in New York State.

Each November, bird watchers can once again see their quarry easily in leafless trees and abandoned nests. This is also a time when snow buntings, true birds of the northern tundra, are easiest to find in open areas along the Hudson. Some birders may spot a rarer visitor from the tundra, a snowy owl. This owl occasionally migrates through our area in winter, showing a preference for treeless spaces of the lower Hudson Valley.

Up above, the Canadian, snow and brant geese will continue to be seen. However, most of the puddle ducks, such as mallards, have left the area. As winter draws closer in upstate New York, we will begin to see winter ducks such as buffleheads, mergansers, goldeneye, canvasbacks, scaup, ring-necked ducks and ruddy ducks.

Bald eagles will follow the diving ducks south, seeking both open water for fishing and the waterfowl themselves to feed upon. Now in the Hudson Valley year-round, the number of bald eagle sightings increase as migrating eagles from the north are seen. Some migrant eagles stay in the Hudson Valley all winter and others will wonder if they should stay or go.

Although the bald eagles grab your attention, you will also see other birds in the sky that migrate in the late fall: rough-legged hawks, red-shouldered hawks, goshawks and golden eagles.

As the river chills into the 50 degree F range, striped bass will start to move into their winter holding areas in the lower Hudson and New York Harbor. The bass seem to sort themselves out according to size and age, with certain areas of the estuary providing a comfort zone for each. There also should be good autumn fishing in the river's Tappan Zee area from Nyack, NY to Fort Lee, NJ for older striped bass, perhaps fish weighing forty pounds or more. Young bass concentrate in New York Harbor their first and second winters and many of these smaller fish shelter among the piers of Manhattan's West Side waterfront. Winter-migratory fish, such as ling and tomcod, can be found and caught in the Hudson areas of Yonkers, Englewood, Alpine or Spuyten Duyvil in Manhattan.

Late November is also the period when blue crabs begin to hunker down for winter. They burrow into the river bottom and enter a torpid state of reduced metabolic activity. Since blue crabs live at the northern end of the species' range, their survival will largely depend upon the severity of the winter. Heavy icing in tidewater can kill many of the young crabs, which are no bigger than a quarter.

During late autumn and winter, life forms in the Hudson prepare their meals for next summer. Aquatic plants are dying back and their discarded leaves join the millions that November rains wash into the Hudson from the land, creating mats of organic matter that float with the tidal currents. This detritus provides fertilizer for the estuary as it is broken down by bacteria and becomes a broth of essential nutrients for plants and microorganisms, flowing through estuarine food chains from plankton, to fish, birds and even to us.

Yet despite what kinds of plants, fish and wildlife that live in or near the Hudson River, pollution problems and solutions have been two big issues for environmentalists and citizens for decades.

By the mid-1950s, the river was a polluted mess as toxic waste and sewage development started to quickly consume what once was flourishing water, farmland and pastures. Hence Hudson River contaminants have sparked river officials to do what they can to improve the water quality of the Hudson River. Although significant progress has been made in cleaning up sewage pollution in the Hudson, problems remain which have to be addressed.

River sewage pollution problems include accidental sewer overflows and sewage discharges during wet weather events and power outages. Overflows occur in many places that have combined sewer and storm drains that flood during periods of heavy rainfall. In addition, increased population along the Hudson River in recent years has pushed existing sewage treatment plants to their maximum capacity and many by the river need to be upgraded. Water pollution comes from other sources in the watershed as well. Oil and gasoline from parking lots, fertilizers from farms and lawns and sediments from construction sites end up in the tributaries and the estuary. In addition, on numerous occasions General Motors, Inc. dumped paint from its old auto plant in Tarrytown, NY into the Hudson River.

Another factor that affects water quality is chemical contaminants in the river.
Contaminants are metals and chemicals that don't break down or break down slowly. Most contaminants in the Hudson are left over from industrial practices, which continued until the 1970s. Contaminants may injure humans, animals, plants and fish. Some of the contaminants (some which I mentioned earlier) in the Hudson River include polychlorinated biphenyls (PCBs), furans, dioxin, heavy metals (lead, copper, zinc, cadmium, chromium and mercury), pesticides and polycyclic aromatic hydrocarbons (PAHs).

PCBs are the most significant pollutants in the Hudson. PCBs are a class of 209 industrial chemicals that are very persistent environmental contaminants. These chemicals were once used by industries, such as General Electric (GE), as insulating fluid in capacitors, transformers and electrical systems. From 1947 to 1977, two GE plants, one at Fort Edward and the other at Hudson Falls, New York, discharged from 500,000 to 1.5 million pounds of PCBs into the upper Hudson. The two GE facilities contaminated over 200 miles of the river from Hudson Falls to the New York Harbor. These PCBs accumulated in sediments and in the bodies of mammals, amphibians, fish and reptiles.

Outside of the GE case, in 1970, environmentalists faced a huge blow when the Federal Power Commission (FPC) decided to grant Con Edison, New York State's main power company, the license for the Storm King, NY plant. But conservationists didn't give up and started to attack the plant project by challenging the water quality permits Con Ed was required to get. By July 1974, a new fishery study prompted the appeals court to order more hearings. Yet during that same period, Con Edison came under new leadership and was willing to reexamine the power plant plan. Finally, in 1980, the company agreed to give up the fight and donated the land purchased for plant construction to be used as a park.

Regarding General Electric (GE), which I just mentioned earlier, in 1977 the federal government banned PCB but the chemical and pesticide DDT are still in the river. Today, over 300,000 pounds of PCBs remain concentrated in the bottom sediments of the river. The spread of PCBs throughout the Hudson River and the food chain it supports have created one of the most extensive hazardous waste problems in the country.

According to the Environmental Protection Agency (EPA), PCBs are a probable human carcinogen. Exposure to PCBs has been linked to a variety of cancers, including biliary tract, liver, skin and brain. Moreover, recent studies have linked PCB exposure to non-cancer health effects, including reproductive failure, birth defects, developmental disorders and impairments to nervous and immune systems. The non-cancer health effects have been seen in both humans and wildlife, appear at low exposure levels and affect the unborn babies and nursing offspring of mothers exposed to PCBs.

Although contaminated fish consumption poses the most potent route of human exposure, local communities are also at some risk from PCB releases into air and from the presence of PCBs in the drinking water supplies of many New York State communities which draw their water from the Hudson River. Today, the New York City watershed is the main source where New York City and New York State residents get their drinking water. The city of New York's watershed encompasses an area of more than 1,900 square miles in the Catskill Mountains and the Hudson Valley. This watershed is divided into two reservoir systems: the Catskill/Delaware watershed located west of the Hudson River and the Croton watershed, located east of the Hudson River. Combined, these reservoir systems deliver about 1.4 billion gallons of water every day to about 9 million people living in New York City, most of Westchester County, and in parts of Orange, Putnam and Ulster counties.

Quality of drinking water is a huge river-related issue that must be resolved. Yet nevertheless, PCBs are still concentrated in the sediments of the river and these contaminants can easily sweep into the water column and spread throughout the course of the river and its ecosystem. EPA experts estimated that over 90% of the PCBs in the water column of the lower Hudson River originate from the 40-mile stretch of the upper Hudson River between Fort Edward and Troy, New York. PCBs from areas of significant accumulation in this region constantly disperse downstream, causing ongoing contamination of the Hudson River Estuary.

Meanwhile, the EPA is currently reconsidering a Superfund cleanup of Hudson River PCB contamination. Under Superfund, a federal program to clean up hazardous waste, GE could be held responsible for its pollution of the river and may have to pay for a comprehensive cleanup.

Cleanup, according to the EPA and the New York State Department of Environmental Conservation (DEC), would consist of the dredging of PCB contaminated sediments that will permanently reduce the transport of PCBs throughout the river that will reduce PCB levels in fish and in the water column. Dredging will also reduce human health risks and will restore our environment. Other good news regarding dredging the Hudson comes from Washington, DC. Although the Hudson River was ranked as the thirty-third most polluted river in the United States, in 2002, the Washington-based American Rivers conservation group dropped the Hudson from the list of America's most endangered rivers after the Environmental Protection Agency (EPA) ruled that General Electric Corporation must dredge the river of PCBs that it dumped there for 30 years.

Regarding dredging, one procedure would entail that contaminated sediments would be removed using a cutterhead auction dredge. Studies indicate that the cutterhead dredge will be more effective than other dredging equipment, with the more operational flexibility and better maneuverability near shorelines. The Hudson River dredging is the biggest project in our nation's history. However, some New York citizens oppose dredging of the Hudson and said it will stir up dormant PCBs, ruin sport fishing, create a lot of sludge with no place to put it and generally shut down the river for years.

In addition to dredging, there are two kinds of safe, effective technologies to treat and destroy PCBs once removed from the riverbed. Separation technologies, which remove PCBs from sediments to produce a smaller volume of more concentrated PCBs and destruction technologies, will break apart PCB molecules. The primary benefit of separation technologies is a huge reduction in the volume of hazardous material.

As long as huge amounts of PCBs are concentrated in upper river sediments, they can be removed from the river. However, as PCB contaminated sediments are scoured up from the riverbed and dispersed, it then becomes almost impossible to recapture them. The longer PCBs remain in the river, the greater the risk a major flood will wash large amounts of PCBs into the lower river. As a result, action needs to be taken as soon as possible.

In addition to PCBs, another source of pollution comes from boats that have discharged human waste into the river. Boat sewage in bodies of water such as the Hudson River can contribute to the whole degradation of marine habitats. It also contains harmful chemicals and bacteria that can damage wetlands, degrade water quality and harm wildlife habitats. But fortunately, New York State's petition to the federal government to make "Vessel No Discharge Zones"(prohibiting boats from dumping waste into the river), combined with funding to provide more pump-out buildings where boat waste can be processed properly, has helped to improve water quality. The 81,000 acres of wetlands and tidal waters lining the Hudson from the Battery to Troy, NY will be the main beneficiaries of the No Discharge Zones. The Environmental Protection Agency (EPA) has already determined that 35 pump-out facilities operating along the 153-mile stretch of the Hudson at yacht clubs, marinas, industrial facilities and other sites is sufficient for the 35,000 or more vessels that sail on the river from the Battery to Troy.

Besides No Discharge Zones, environmentalists have recently claimed that dams in the Hudson River have damaged river life. And according to environmental experts and state regulators, many of these dams that were built for flood control, navigation and hydroelectric power generation, are now crippled and need to be removed from the Hudson River watershed. River experts claimed that eventually, a free-flowing stream or free-flowing "Hudson River tributary" is preferred because derelict dams will fall apart in time from floods without ongoing maintenance. Moreover, with dams in place, sections of streams become lake-like, changing the flow of sediment, nutrients, dissolved oxygen and even warmth. Regarding sediment, dams slow the water so much that sediment settles behind dams instead of mixing in the water and flowing downstream. Dammed water also heats up in the summer and as it spills downstream, it is often hot enough to shock cold-water species such as trout. Dissolved oxygen that is needed for fish and other aquatic life is also decreased as it runs downstream over the dam. Dams also alter chemistry and put a physical barrier in the way of fish. Ocean-dwelling migratory fish that spawn in streams, such as river herring and American shad, are affected, as are American eels that spawn in the ocean but grow to adulthood in streams. In some streams where the first barrier to fish is a manmade dam, as opposed to a natural waterfall, fish are blocked from historic spawning grounds. Dams also affect resident fish and other living things that don't migrate to oceans. Environmentalists have now proposed three ways to restore damaged waterways connecting the Hudson River. One way is to remove the dam completely. The problem with that way is once the dam is gone, wetlands and the habitat it provided will be destroyed. Another way is to dig a new channel around the dam. The third method would be to build a fish passage device. These don't restore the river continuum (dams & other barriers on the tributaries of the Hudson River estuary block) but help with fish migration. Fish elevators, fish ladders and rock ramps allow fish to move up the river, but not all of these are simple to navigate, depending on how agile a particular fish species is.

In addition to No Discharge Zones and proposed solutions to problems that dams can cause to the river's ecosystem, more projects are now underway to upgrade water quality in the New York Harbor, which is now cleaner than it has been in the past fifty years. These New York City-related water projects range from the removal of floating debris in storm sewers to improvements within water pollution control plants.

Moreover, according to a recent report made by the Hudson River Foundation (New York City-based organization that conducts science & environmental research on the Hudson River), the environmental health of the New York City Harbor has improved as much as ten-fold in the past thirty years. The Foundation's "Health of the Harbor" Report is prepared for the New York/New Jersey Harbor Estuary Program. This scientific report examines the environmental conditions of the Hudson Estuary and looks at environmental trends. The Foundation also closely monitors key scientific and environmental indicators over time throughout the New York Harbor.

Regarding the environment, conservation experts also point out that more research needs to be done on pier, platform areas, and their habitat values. The experts also stated that they would need time to completely understand the relationships of the river's physical environment, inwater and shoreline structures, seasonal salinity and temperature regimes, and the habitat values resulting from these interactions. Conservationists state that Piermont Marsh, one of the four sites in the Hudson River National Estuarine Research Reserve, should be the focus of monitored restoration efforts, including restoration of diamondback terrapin nesting areas.

Furthermore, the U.S. Army Corps of Engineers, along with the New York State Department of State and the New York State Department of Environmental Conservation, has a habitat restoration study and project underway in the Hudson basin. The project will probably result in restoration of areas affected by past dredging projects, including enhancing circulation to tidal marsh areas, control and removal of exotic species, and creation of more marsh areas. As part of this study, fifteen sites were identified as priority restoration locations, including three sites in the lower Hudson: Piermont Marsh, Croton Bay to New York Harbor and Spuyten Duyvil. Meanwhile, establishing more open space by the tributaries and along the Hudson as part of the Hudson Valley Greenway will increase the riparian habitat and provide greater appreciation for this important resource.

Today, the Hudson Estuary program continues to examine contaminant levels in mink, muskrat, reptiles, amphibians, insects and other species. It has made a long-time commitment to reduce contaminants in the Hudson by tracking them and determining which contaminants are discovered in the river, where they are located and where they are coming from. Obviously, the clean-up of the Hudson River is essential if we want to continue using all of its resources.

Clean-up is the key solution to reduce pollutants in the river and on its shoreline. To help in this cleanup effort, Scenic Hudson, Inc., a Poughkeepsie, NY-based conservation group, organizes its Great River Sweep event each spring. During this annual sweep, thousands of volunteers pick up garbage and assist with cleaning the Hudson River's tributaries, shorelines, and public places from Manhattan to Albany.

In fact, today the Hudson cleanup has been so successful that residents of Poughkeepsie are taking drinking water from the river and the number of swimmers in the Hudson has steadily increased. In 2001, 1,976 swimmers participated in eight races, the largest number in more than 50 years. Hardly anyone would have dreamed of diving into the river water during the 1970s. The '70s was a decade when the Hudson River was ranked the second most contaminated huge estuary in America with metals, including copper and mercury.

Nevertheless, the cleanup of the river has been so successful that the state of New York has designated the areas north of Manhattan as safe for swimming, its highest ranking. State experts ranked the south section, from the Harlem River to the Battery, as safe for fishing, the second-cleanest ranking. Alex Matthiessen, director of Riverkeeper (a New York-based environmental organization), said the key to the improved water quality throughout the estuary was the federal Clean Water Act of 1972. The Clean Water Act prohibited businesses (from junkyards to Con Edison & General Electric) that were discharging oil, debris and toxic chemicals and gave citizens the right to sue polluters. "Until then, the river was one of the most polluted waterways in the country," Matthiessen said. According to Department of Environmental Protection officials, the Hudson River is the cleanest it's been in 90 to 100 years.

Indeed cleanup does improve river water quality; however, the present condition of the Hudson River remains unclear. Some people state that the Hudson (along with its fauna and flora) is co-existing wonderfully. Others state that the continuing problems with pollutants (PCBs and thermal energy) still affect the Hudson. The river does have pollution problems, but nonetheless it is recovering. In 1995, a Superfund cleanup removed cadmium-laden sediments (the main source of metal pollution into the Hudson) in Foundry Cove near Cold Spring, NY. That particular cleanup of Foundry Cove will decrease the transfer of metals through the river's food webs. In addition to the Superfund cleanup, on July 30, 1998, another pollution solution emerged as President Clinton then recognized the Hudson River (one of ten rivers in the U.S.) as an American Heritage River guaranteeing New York State and local governments with federal protection and funding for the Hudson River.

However, when it comes to pollution cleanup, it's still difficult to keep the Hudson completely clean. Furthermore, constant vigilance is required now and in the future to prevent environmental backsliding. Unfortunately, the recent invasion of zebra mussels has resulted in large declines in freshwater phytoplankton and noticeable decreases in oxygen. Before the mussels, mislead introductions of organisms like common carp, water chestnut and others have had negative effects in portions of the estuary and these mistakes typically are irreversible. And although pollution inputs have been decreased tremendously, intermittent episodes may still happen, such as oil spills. In addition, non-point sources of contaminants still leach into the Hudson River's ecosystem.

Yet regardless of which sections of the river are polluted, the health of Hudson River residents is another important issue. Fortunately, there's some good news for riverside residents. Recent studies completed in 2006 indicated that compared to other New

York State residents, residents of the Hudson River got more exercise and ate more fruits and vegetables, both which show indirect results of the incidence of obesity. Furthermore, the current smoking rates along the Hudson River are less than the rest of the state and residents of the areas along the contaminated portion of the river have higher average incomes; there are fewer families with incomes less than $24,999 and more families with incomes exceeding $50,000. So the bottom line is that Hudson River residents smoke less, live a healthier lifestyle, and have higher incomes than other New Yorkers.

Hudson River Photos

Photo taken by F. C. Shipley of the Dobbs Ferry Hudson River Landing in 1955. Courtesy of the Dobbs Ferry Historical Society in Dobbs Ferry, New York.

A replica of Henry Hudson's *Half Moon* which classified as a sloop. Courtesy of Croton Historical Society in Croton on the Hudson, New York.

A small steamboat which looked like a floating grocery store. Courtesy of Croton Historical Society in Croton on the Hudson, New York.

The sloop *Clearwater* and environmental awareness replica started by singer and activist, Pete Seeger. Courtesy of Croton Historical Society in Croton on the Hudson, New York.

The Fort Lee Ferry. Courtesy of Fort Lee Historical Society in Fort Lee, New Jersey.

The steam boat *Henrick Hudson* which ran as an excursion boat on the Hudson. Courtesy of Croton Historical Society in Croton on the Hudson, New York.

This photo is circa 1930. It shows the *William Strong* hosing the dock at Anaconda Wire & Cable Company, which was located at the Hudson River waterfront in Hastings-on-Hudson, New York. Courtesy of Hastings Historical Society in Hastings-on-the-Hudson, New York.

This photo shows catboats on the Hudson River before a race at Tower Ridge Yacht Club in Hastings-on-Hudson, New York. This photo was taken in 1893. Courtesy of Hastings Historical Society in Hastings-on-the-Hudson, New York.

Hudson River postcard: Hudson River, showing Lighthouse and Maxwell Briscoe Factory, Tarrytown, New York. Courtesy of the Westchester County Historical Society in Elmsford, New York.

Hudson River postcard: "Indian Head," highest point (510 ft.) of Palisades, Hudson River. Courtesy of the Westchester County Historical Society in Elmsford, New York.

Hudson River postcard: "Anthony's Nose," Hudson River, Highlands. Courtesy of Westchester County Historical Society in Elmsford, New York.

Hudson River postcard: South from Bear Mountain, Hudson River, New York. Courtesy of Westchester County Historical Society in Elmsford, New York.

Trolley. Courtesy of Fort Lee Historical Society in Fort Lee, New Jersey.

Fort Lee Fishermans Village. Courtesy of Fort Lee Historical Society in Fort Lee, New Jersey.

This photo is of a steam-engine train heading south from the Hastings-on-Hudson, New York station on the Hudson River line. The photo shows the Hastings Train Station in the center behind the train and Southside Avenue on the right. The photo was taken sometime before 1910. Courtesy of Hastings Historical Society in Hastings-on-the-Hudson, New York.

The Anaconda Wire & Cable Company Water Tower is located on the Hudson River waterfront in Hastings-on-Hudson, New York. Anaconda is a company that is no longer in existence, but that once employed hundreds of Hastings blue-collar workers in the middle of the last century. This photo, which is from 1983, shows Palisades, New Jersey in the background. The water tower—a bit more faded—is still standing to this day. Courtesy of Hastings Historical Society in Hastings-on-the-Hudson, New York.

The Newburgh Steam Mills factory (plant) was built in 1825. Courtesy of Newburgh Historical Society in Newburgh, New York.

Hudson River postcard: Hudson River, Yonkers, New York. Courtesy of Westchester County Historical Society in Elmsford, New York.

Hudson River by Riparius in the southern Adirondacks, New York. Photo by Carl Heilman.

George Washington Bridge. Photo by Carl Heilman.

Bear Mountain Bridge from the Route 9 bridge near Fort Montgomery, New York. Photo by Carl Heilman.

Hudson River just north of North Creek, New York—fly fishing. Photo by Carl Heilman.

Hudson River—Rockwell Falls from the Hadley Luzerne bridge, New York. Photo by Carl Heilman.

Inwood Hill Park Preserve views over the Hudson River to the Palisades of New Jersey. Photo by Carl Heilman.

Croton Point Park—looking south over the Hudson River Tappan Zee area, New York to the Palisades of New Jersey. Photo by Carl Heilman.

Chapter 3
Hudson River Access/Transportation Links
(Railroads, Recreation & Commercial Vessels, Bridges, Tunnels, etc.)

You can best see the beauty of the Hudson River and its banks by riding on a train, bus or sailing on a cruise line ship.

Railroads that operate in New York and offer visitors a good view of the Hudson and its surrounding areas are the Metro-North Railroad and Amtrak.

The Metro-North Railroad, which originates from Grand Central Station in Manhattan, serves points on the East Side of the Hudson River. Metro North's Hudson Line provides service to all the Hudson River towns of the lower Hudson Valley from Yonkers north to Croton-on-the-Hudson. North of Croton, train station stops are found in Cortlandt, Peekskill, Manitou, Garrison, Cold Spring, Breakneck Ridge, Beacon and New Hamburg. The last Metro-North train stop is located in Poughkeepsie, north of New Hamburg. Then north of Poughkeepsie, Amtrak has trains that continue to roll north to and beyond Albany.

Amtrak's Empire Corridor trains also give riders opportunities to get scenic views of the Hudson River. Amtrak offers travelers a train trip along the east bank of the Hudson River from New York City to the Albany/Renesselaer, NY area that is one of the most scenic trains trips in the United States. Amtrak provides service from New York City's Penn Station (in Manhattan) to New York State communities which include Yonkers, Croton-Harmon, Poughkeepsie, Rhinecliff/Kingston, Hudson, Albany/Rensselaer, Schenectady and Saratoga Springs.

Besides Metro-North and Amtrak, for those who wish to see points of interest on the west side of the Hudson River, people can catch the New Jersey Transit/Metro North Railroad. The New Jersey Transit/Metro North Railroad provides service from Penn Station north to New York State regions that include Rockland County, Harriman, Newburgh and Middletown.

And for visitors wanting to ride the rails to get a close glimpse of the Upper Hudson area, the Upper Hudson River Railroad will accommodate them. The Hudson River Railroad has scenic trains that offer passengers a great view of the Adirondack Mountains and the Hudson River. The Upper Hudson River Railroad operates seasonal 2-hour round-trip excursions along an 8.5-mile section of the former Adirondack Branch of the D&H Railroad.

The trains board passengers from restored platforms of the North Creek Depot and Freight House and then as the trip progresses, sightseers will enjoy a 30-minute layover at the Riverside Station, located on the banks of the Hudson River and surrounded by the Adirondack Mountains. Once at Riverside Station, riders will enjoy the historic displays in the station, Riverside Park and can proceed over a Walking Bridge, which will take them over the Hudson River.

In addition to trains, travelers interested in viewing scenic areas along the Hudson can ride the bus. Bus service throughout the Hudson Valley is available on Adirondack/Pine Hills Trailways with service to New York City, New Paltz, Kingston and Albany while both Greyhound Bus Lines and Shortline Coach USA provide local service from New York City and throughout Orange, Rockland and Dutchess counties.

Besides train and bus trips, cruise line ships offer sightseers scenic views of the Hudson and its surrounding areas. Ten popular cruise lines are the New Hudson River Day Line, Hudson Highlands Cruises & Tours, Hudson River Adventures, Hudson River Cruises, North River Cruises, River Valley Tours, Abenaki, Eastern Star Cruises, American Cruise Lines and River Rose.

The New Hudson River Day Line departs from Pier 81 in Manhattan on Saturdays and Sundays at 9:30 a.m. During the season (May 25 to September 15), the Day Line makes trips to Poughkeepsie (nonstop) via Bear Mountain and West Point, NY. The boat arrives back at the pier in Manhattan on both Saturday and Sunday at 6:30 p.m.

Hudson Highland Cruises features the M/V *Commander*, a classic excursion boat out of Haverstraw, NY which plies the Hudson from May through October, serving charter groups and offering cruises from New York State's West Haverstraw to West Point and Bannerman's Island. On the last Saturday of the month, a 3-hour narrated cruise north to Hudson Highlands also leaves from Peekskill's Riverfront Green. The M/V *Commander* is an historic vessel and has a certified captain and crew. Ample seating is available on the upper deck, with a canopy to afford both sun and shade. The Commander offers a fully licensed bar and can cater a range of food, from simple picnic fare to gourmet dinners.

The third Hudson Cruise Line is Hudson River Adventures (also called *Pride of the Hudson*), which is known to be the most elegant ship in the Hudson Valley. The cruise liner begins its journey out of Newburgh Landing in Newburgh, NY, on the river's western banks. Passengers can enjoy its fully enclosed, climate-controlled, main deck while enjoying the majestic panorama of the river and the valley as seen through large wrap-around windows. Riders can also enjoy the passing scenery from the spacious sundeck, topside. A fully licensed captain and courteous crew operate the *Pride of the Hudson* and narrated sightseeing cruises are offered on Wednesdays, Fridays, Saturdays and Sundays.

Another river cruise line is Hudson River Cruises, which is a 300-passenger vessel that is a great way to see the river. This vessel combines the gracious pace of the Old World with all the comforts of today. This ship houses a snack bar and fully stocked bar where passengers can relax on a cool, shaded deck with a lunch while their guide offers a capsule history of the legendary Hudson River Valley, pointing out its beautiful sights. Different departures leave from Rondout Landing at the foot of Broadway in Kingston, NY. Hudson River Cruises offers daily two-hour sightseeing trips, sunset sip n' sails and dance cruises. Private charters and group discounts are also available.

The fifth Hudson River Cruise Line is called North River Cruises which features the Motor Yacht *Teal*, with Captain John M. Cutten, which takes passengers back to the time of simple elegance and genteel river travel with all the amenities of a modern vessel. *Teal's* staff customizes excursions to and from a variety of ports and offers private and corporate charters, including weddings, graduations and family gatherings. Live entertainment and sunset dance cruises also are offered, while the food and beverage service can fit anyone's budget. The *Teal*, whose homeport is the historic Rondout district of Kingston, is certified and inspected by the U.S. Coast Guard.

River Valley Tours is another Hudson Cruise that features *The Crescent*, the 63-foot vessel that takes passengers from New

York City north to Albany. The ship makes stops on its trip so those passengers can take in historical sights along the way. Guests spend the night on land, sleeping in some of the best hotels in the Hudson Valley, including the famous Hotel Thayer located at West Point Military Academy. Visits to Hyde Park and the home of Franklin D. Roosevelt, Vanderbilt Mansion and the Mohonk Mountain House are a few of the highlights of the trip, ending with tours in Albany and Troy. A bus returns to New York City for those who need to return at the end of the week. In addition, this cruise liner hosts the only tour that explores the entire Hudson Valley, from the shore as well as from the water.

Abenaki is yet another vessel that sails on the Hudson. The *Abenaki* recaptures the quiet, smooth and peaceful feel of the motor vessel touring once common on the Hudson but now almost forgotten. Her name comes from Native Americans whose name means "the dawn land people." The *Abenaki's* air-conditioned main cabin features huge windows, comfortable seating and a large dining table. The aft deck is a canopied semicircle with upholstered perimeter seating. The vessel's passenger list is limited to six people for each cruise, departing May through October from Upper Nyack. Departures and arrivals may be made from a variety of ports on the lower Hudson River by special request.

The eighth Hudson Cruise is called Eastern Star Cruises which charters the Motor Yacht *Eastern Star*, also known as the Cruising Country Inn. Unlike a dinner cruise vessel, the *Eastern Star* offers passengers an elegant "inn-like" atmosphere. Designed with casual elegance in mind, her climate-controlled interior boasts rich mahogany, gleaming brass, plush furnishings and a wood-burning stove that glows on cooler days and evenings. Both main and upper decks are fully carpeted and feature mahogany bars and stereo sound systems. Leisurely day or overnight excursions take you through the Hudson River Valley, Cold Spring, West Point, Hyde Park, Bannerman Island and Kingston which provide a dramatic backdrop for exploring historical landmarks, hiking or just relaxing. *Eastern Star* is also available for family gatherings, weddings and corporate events. The ship is United States Coast Guard-approved for 49-day passengers or 10 overnight passengers and offers convenient pickup locations in the New York City area or from Haverstraw, NY.

Then there's American Cruise Lines, which offers eight-day cruises up the Hudson River, embarking from Hadden, Connecticut. Passengers can enjoy fine dining, gorgeous foliage and the sounds of summer while being pampered aboard the new, 31-stateroom *American Eagle*. As one of only 49 passengers you will embark on an 8-day, 7-night cruise beginning on the Connecticut River, continuing up the historic Hudson. Your six points of call include West Point, Kingston and New York City where you will be able to participate in specially planned ashore tours.

The tenth Hudson Cruise is the *River Rose*, an authentic paddle wheeler, which takes passengers sailing into the history of Bannerman's Island. During fall foliage cruises, sightseers will marvel at the spectrum and slender of the colors of Breakneck and Storm King Mountains and the magnificent palaces built on the Hudson River in the past century. The *River Rose* accommodates up to 150 passengers and there are air conditioned upper and lower decks for your viewing convenience. In addition, light snacks are available at the full-service bars and private charters are available for corporate to birthday parties.

No matter if it's for business or pleasure, traveling by train or ship on the Hudson represents reliable and scenic modes of transportation for the public. Yet besides railroads and cruise liners, many commuters rely on bridges and tunnels to get them across or under the river. In fact, there's more than a half a dozen bridges which cross the Hudson. Perhaps the most famous bridge in America is the George Washington Bridge (GWB). The George Washington is the most heavily used bridge in the world, with about 300,000 crossings a day. This span connects 179th St. in Manhattan, New York with Fort Lee, New Jersey. This bridge towers over the Hudson allowing motorists to reach their New York and/or New Jersey destinations.

The height of the George Washington's tower above the river water is 604 feet. On the New Jersey side, the tower rises out of the river 76 feet from shore; on the New York side, the tower stands on land. The bridge's width is 119 feet and the length of the span between anchorages is 4,760 feet. The bridge's water clearance at mid-span is 212 feet.

Two 3-lane approach and departure roadways serve the Lower Level, with connections to and from the GWB via two 3-lane tunnels through the Palisades. Two 4-lane approach and departure roadways connect to the Upper Level. The Upper Level is suspended from four steel cables, each 36 inches in diameter and composed of 26,474 wires. Saddles on top of two 604-foot-high steel towers carry the cables. On both levels of the bridge, the New Jersey approaches include US-1, US-46, US-9W, NJ-4, I-80, I-95 and the Palisades Interstate Parkway.

Another Hudson River Bridge, located about 25 miles north of midtown Manhattan, is the Governor Malcolm Wilson Tappan Zee Bridge, mostly referred to as the Tappan Zee Bridge. The Tappan Zee connects Nyack in Rockland County, NY with Tarrytown in Westchester County, NY. The Manhattan skyline can also be seen from the span on a clear day.

The total length of the Tappan Zee and approaches is 16,013 feet (just over 3 miles) and the cantilever span is 1,212 feet and provides a 138-foot clearance over the water. The Tappan Zee is part of the New York State Thruway mainline and also designated as Interstate 87 and Interstate 287. The span carries seven lanes of automotive traffic, with the center lane being switchable between eastbound and westbound traffic depending on the prevalent commuter direction. On business days, the center lane is eastbound in the morning and westbound in the evening.

In addition to its Hudson River transportation link, the Tappan Zee Bridge and Peregrine Falcons have a mutual beneficial relationship. During the late 1980s, the New York Thruway added two falcon-nesting boxes to the Tappan Zee. The boxes, which are located up on the main truss, give falcons a high perch and great views of the Hudson River. At the same time, the falcons keep pigeons away from the bridge. Pigeon droppings are detrimental to the paint and the steel on the bridge. Before the nesting boxes were added, many pigeons roosted on the bridge. Falcon-nesting boxes have also been added to a few other NY Thruway Authority bridges which include the Castleton Bridge, a one-mile bridge which spans the Hudson River about ten miles south of Albany.

Besides the Tappan Zee Bridge and other small spans located near it, as you travel further north across the Hudson, you'll find Bear Mountain Bridge. The span, another toll suspension bridge in New York State, carries two lanes of U.S. Highways 202 and 6, as well as the Appalachian Trial, across the Hudson River between Rockland and Orange Counties to the west and Westchester and Putnam Counties to the east. The bridge allows connections to the Palisades Interstate Parkway and U.S. Highway 9W on the West Bank of the Hudson to New York State Route 9D on the east side.

When Bear Mountain Bridge opened on November 27, 1924, it was the first highway bridge to cross the Hudson River south of Albany, New York and the biggest suspension bridge in the world; it was also the first suspension bridge to have a concrete deck. The original construction methods used in building the bridge also made possible several large projects to follow which include the George Washington Bridge.

In addition to Bear Mountain Bridge, there's the Hamilton Fish Newburgh-Beacon Bridge, named after Hamilton Fish, former governor of New York. The Newburgh-Beacon is a two-span, cantilever toll bridge that spans the Hudson in New York State carrying NY 52 and I-84 between Newburgh and Beacon.

Regarding the Newburgh-Beacon's spans the westbound span carries one lane of traffic in each direction. Today, it accommodates three 12-foot travel lanes with no shoulders. Variable lane-use signs allow the right lane to be designated as a breakdown lane at night and off-peak travel times. When the right lane is being used as a shoulder, a red X appears on the signs above it, while a green arrow illuminates when the lane is used for travel during peak times. The newer eastbound span was built with three 12-foot travel lanes, a 10-foot right shoulder, a 6-foot left shoulder and pedestrian sidewalk separated from the roadway by a concrete barrier. Since there are shoulders in this span, it is not necessary to reduce the travel lanes to two during off-peak hours.

The Newburgh-Beacon Bridge provides connections to the New York State Thruway (Interstate 87) via US 9W in Newburgh and US 9 in Fishkill. The bridge includes a 2,204-foot cantilever span, with a main span of 1,000 feet and side spans of 602 feet. The total length of all spans and approaches is 7,855 feet for the north span and 7,789 feet for the south span.

Moving along the Hudson we come to the Franklin D. Roosevelt Mid-Hudson Bridge, a toll bridge which carries US 44 and NY 55 across the river in New York State. The bridge is officially named in memory of Franklin D. Roosevelt, who was governor of New York at the time the bridge opened in 1930. The span connects Poughkeepsie and Highland and is often referred to as the "Mid-Hudson Bridge" as opposed to the Franklin D. Roosevelt Mid-Hudson Bridge.

This suspension bridge is 3,000 feet long and has a clearance of 135 feet above the Hudson. What makes this bridge unlike most others is that the stiffening trusses were intentionally constructed on top of, not below the deck.

Today, the Mid-Hudson Bridge carries three lanes and a pedestrian/bicycle walkway over the Hudson. The center lane is almost always closed and mostly used for rush hour traffic eastbound from 6 a.m. to 9 a.m. and westbound from 3 p.m. to 6 p.m. Variable signs at either foot of the bridge are used to indicate lane closures, as both approaches are four lanes wide. This system is similar to that of the Newburgh-Beacon Bridge about 20 miles to the south. The bridge has a computer-controlled LED decorative lighting system attached to the suspension cables, allowing the bridge to be decorated for Christmas (red, green) or the Fourth of July (red, white and blue), etc.

Besides the Mid-Hudson Bridge, there's the Kingston-Rhinecliff Bridge in New York State. This span is 7,793 feet long and is a continuous under-deck truss bridge that crosses the Hudson north of the City of Kingston and the hamlet of Rhinecliff.

This toll bridge carries two lanes of traffic with shoulders and about 17,000 vehicles per day travel on it. The Kingston-Rhinecliff has two main spans since there is an east and west channel in the Hudson River at this point. It also has a clearance over 250 feet above the river.

Yet another bridge which crosses the Hudson is the Rip Van Winkle Bridge. The bridge is named after the short story of the same name by Washington Irving. The Rip Van Winkle is a cantilever bridge spanning the Hudson River between Hudson and Catskill, New York. The structure carries NY 23 across the river, connecting on the west side with US 9W and NY 385 with NY 9G on the east side. The length of the main span is 800 feet; it extends 5,040 feet across the river and provides a ship clearance of 145 feet.

The last two Hudson River Bridges I just wanted to briefly mention is the NY Thruway (I-90-I87) Bridge that connects I87 at exit 21A with the Berl section of I90 (to Boston), just south of Albany, NY. The second Hudson Bridge that crosses the river is the I90 Bridge in Albany.

Bridges are effective structures, which provide people the means to cross the Hudson River. But you can also get from one side to another under the river and that's where tunnels come into the picture.

Perhaps the most well-known highway tunnels for motorists are the Lincoln and Holland Tunnels.

The Lincoln Tunnel beneath the Hudson connecting NJ 495 in Weehawken, New Jersey with NY 495 in Manhattan (New York City). It carries about 120,000 vehicles per day, making it one of the busiest vehicular tunnels in the world. The tunnel also provides a lane for buses on weekday mornings, which by far is the busiest bus lane in the United States. The tunnel is made up of three tubes that hold a total of six lanes of traffic. The North Tube is 7,482 feet long, the Center Tube is 8,216 feet long and the length of the South Tube is 8,006 feet. The tunnel's width is 21.5 feet and its vertical clearance measures 13 feet.

The Holland Tunnel is a four-lane passageway under the Hudson connecting Manhattan with Jersey City, New Jersey at Interstate 78 on the mainland. The tunnel consists of two tubes, each providing two lanes in a twenty-foot roadway width. The South Tube is 8,371 feet long and the length of the North Tube is 8,558 feet. Both tubes are located in the bedrock under the river, with the lowest point of the roadway about 93 feet below mean high water. The structure's vertical clearance is 12 feet 6 inches. In addition, a nine-lane toll plaza equipped with E-ZPass is located on the New Jersey side of the tunnel.

In addition to the historic, vehicular tunnels, the Port Authority of New York & New Jersey and the New Jersey Transit have plans for a new train tunnel. The new passageway will be named the Trans-Hudson Express Tunnel. The Trans-Hudson is a proposed railroad tunnel that would be built under the Hudson River, connecting Palisades, New Jersey with midtown Manhattan, New York.

This new tunnel would add transportation capacity to the existing two-track railroad tunnels under the Hudson, the North River Tunnels, used by Amtrak and New Jersey Transit, that are already operating under full capacity. This huge project is slated to begin construction by 2010 and for completion in 2016 or 2017, at the earliest. Transportation officials project that rail ridership between New Jersey and Midtown Manhattan will double to 100,000 rush-hour passengers daily by 2015.

Plans for the tunnel would include two new tracks under the Hudson River and the New Jersey Palisades and a new six-track passenger station under 34th Street connecting with Penn Station in Manhattan. There will also be plans for improvements in New Jersey to provide a one-seat ride to Midtown Manhattan (for New Jersey Transit riders on the Raritan Valley Line, Main Line/Bergen County Line & Pascack Valley Line) and a rail storage yard in Kearny, New Jersey.

Also in New Jersey, the Hudson-Bergen Light Rail (HBLR), a light rail system owned by New Jersey Transit and operated by the 21st Century Rail Corporation, is a 20.6-mile rail line that connects the cities of Bayonne, Jersey City, Hoboken, Weehawken, Union City and North Bergen in New Jersey. The HBLR was put in place for this densely populated area in order to relieve increasing congestion along the Hudson River waterfront, particularly in the area of the Hudson River crossings.

In addition to cruise ships, trains, tunnels and bridges, the commercial maritime industry, especially in New York Harbor, represents the Hudson as a "working river" that supports the overall economy of New York and New Jersey. Every day, several thousand large ships visit the New York Harbor. There are about 750 tugs and barges (note: tug & barge combinations can weigh up to 10,700 tons) that transports a variety of construction materials, goods and fuels within the harbor and between coastal points. In addition, the port is home to many other vessels: sludge boats that haul residue from sewage treatment plants for processing; ferries that transport over 100,000 passengers daily for commuting; many excursion vessels (police, fire, pilot, coast guard & navy) and historic ships. Other ships that visit the Port of New York include oil tankers, container ships, auto ships and bulk carriers.

Today, for commercial ships to travel on the Hudson, the river must maintain a minimum depth of about forty feet. The United States Coast Guard is responsible for ensuring safe passage for both commercial and recreational ships traveling on the Hudson. Over 50 years ago, the U.S. Army Corps of Engineers started to dredge portions of the river (lengths of dredged river are called "reaches") to meet commercial vessel depth requirements. Furthermore, commercial vessels have the right of way over all recreational boats.

Chapter 4
Hudson River Historical Attractions/Recreational Activities and Sites

The Hudson River has been blessed with natural scenery on both sides of it. Yet what symbolizes the river and its valley's long history is not trees or plant life but its geology.

In fact, the Black Rock Forest, which is located at the intersection of two main geological features, the New York-New Jersey Highlands and the Hudson River Basin, represents the region's ancient history.

Black Rock Forest has some of the oldest rock in New York State. The gneiss bedrock is a metamorphic rock from the Precambrian age that ranges from 1.1 to 1.3 billion years old. Black Rock Forest is home to many kinds of gneiss. Gneiss is made of the minerals such as quartz, feldspar, amphibole, pyroxene, mica and magnetite.

A series of three significant geologic events uplifted these gneiss rocks to make mountains in New York and weathering and erosion affected the mountains after each mountain-building event. The first event, 440 to 460 million years ago during the Ordovician period, was caused by a collision with an arc-shaped set of volcanic islands east of North America. This event created the New York-New Jersey Highlands. The second event, 335 to 375 million years ago, was caused by a collision with a continent located east of North America. The third event, about 250 million years ago, was caused by a collision with West Africa and it created the continent Pangaea. Approximately 200 million years ago, Pangaea started to split apart and form the continents we know today.

The Adirondack and Catskill Mountains in northern New York were also created by the three events that I mentioned in the last paragraph. In fact, the Hudson River watershed (includes regions from the Adirondacks and upstate New York down to the Atlantic) has also contributed toward the creation of Black Rock Forest. The Hudson and its tributaries are consistently carving away at the land to make the landscape we see in the Hudson River Valley region today.

And as for its name, Black River Forest, it was derived from the mineral magnetite (iron ore) that can be found throughout the Forest. This iron ore, identified by its low melting point, can be extracted from rocks by heating them in a furnace. This liquid iron can also be poured into molds which once made tools, guns and cannons that were used during the Revolutionary War period.

In addition to geology embedded near the Hudson River, the river is also home to quite a few lighthouses. You don't have to go to the shore of the Atlantic Ocean to see those structures. The Hudson River coast is home to seven houses of light. These lighthouses are Hudson-Athens, Saugerties, Rondout, Esopus, Stony Point, Sleepy Hollow and Little Red. Today, the Hudson-Athens Lighthouse serves as navigation, guiding ships safely around the river. Since its opening in 1874 with Henry D. Best as its first keeper, this lighthouse has been operated and maintained by the United States Coast Guard until July, 2000 when the US Coast Guard officially transferred its deed to the Hudson/Athens Lighthouse Preservation Society, Inc. (a nonprofit organization).

The Society is presently responsible for the preservation, restoration and maintenance of the lighthouse while the US Coast Guard is still responsible for operation of the Hudson-Athens Lighthouse's lighted beacon.

Saugerties Lighthouse has been directing ships and navigation on the Hudson River since 1869. This lighthouse is unique in that it's the only one on the Hudson that welcomes overnight guests and it is the only one you can see over land. The lighthouse is furnished like it would look like around 1920. Visiting Saugerties Lighthouse is an educational experience. You can walk to and around the lighthouse at any time.

The trip to the Light Tower is the high point of the visit for most people. From the tower, you have a great view of the Hudson River with the Catskill Mountains to the West and can see the Kingston/Rhinecliff Bridge to the South. The lighthouse is also an excellent site to visit by boats where larger ones can tie up at the floating dock.

Another house of light is called the Rondout Lighthouse, which has been owned by the City of Kingston, New York since 2002. Today, the Hudson River Maritime Museum located in the Rondout section of Kingston maintains the building.

Even though it is now uninhabited, the lighthouse is still a navigational aid to boaters as it stands as a guiding guard at the mouth of the Rondout Creek. The lighthouse brings back memories of sailing ships and paddle wheel steamboats transporting cargo and passengers from the Kingston/Rondout area.

Today, Rondout Lighthouse has period furnishings and exhibits documenting the history of the lighthouses and its keepers on the Rondout. The first lighthouse was made in 1837 but later was damaged by bad weather; it was replaced in 1867. The original keeper, James McCausland, watched the house from March 1838 until December 1838.

The lighthouse is presently open for public visiting from May through October. That's when people can climb the tower and walk on the outdoor platform taking in a great view of the Hudson and Rondout harbor.

Unlike the other Hudson River lighthouses, today, the Esopus Meadows Lighthouse is not open for visitors because it is structurally unsafe. Only recently has the major work of preserving and restoring the lighthouse has begun. To continue repairing the structure, the transfer of ownership from the U.S. Coast Guard to a nonprofit organization must take place. The Coast Guard took over its operations in 1939.

The Esopus Lighthouse was and is strictly accessible by water only. Built in 1838, the U.S. Government allocated $6,000 to build the lighthouse in order to warn ships of the dangerous flats lying between the lighthouse and the shore. The end of the 1860s created a better foundation made of cut stone created to protect the lighthouse from ice and flooding.

Esopus Meadows was originally constructed as a "family lighthouse" where the keeper and his family lived within its structure. In addition, Esopus Meadows Lighthouse is the only existing lighthouse made with a wood frame and clapboard exterior. All the lighthouses of similar construction on the Hudson have disappeared long ago.

The oldest lighthouse on the Hudson River is the Stony Point Lighthouse built in 1826. The first keeper was Cornelius W. Lansing who watched the house from 1826 to 1829.

In 1925, the original lighthouse was decommissioned and replaced by a steel light tower erected near the shore. The light tower was operated manually until the U.S. Coast Guard automated it in 1973. In 1986, the exterior of the lighthouse was painted, repaired and its lantern reglazed. In 1995, the inside of the lighthouse was restored, period lenses with an exhibit were installed and the structure was reopened to the public. Today, public tours of the Stony Point Lighthouse are available regularly on weekends from April to October at the Stony Point Battlefield State Historic Site in Stony Point, New York.

Another lighthouse on the Hudson River is the Sleepy Hollow Lighthouse also known as the Tarrytown Lighthouse built in 1883. This lighthouse was originally erected to be a navigational aid to shipping on the Hudson and it warned captains away from dangerous shoals on the river's eastern shore.

The lighthouse is best viewed from Kingsland Point Park in Sleepy Hollow and it is now open for group tours by appointment only. However, the lighthouse was nearly demolished in 1961 when it became deactivated and the building was listed with the General Services Administration (GSA) for disposal. To make matters worse, when the Tappan Zee Bridge was built in 1955, bridge officials rendered the lighthouse obsolete.

However, thanks to individuals and organizations that wanted to save the Tarrytown Lighthouse, the Westchester County Board of Supervisors voted to accept the lighthouse from the GSA in 1969. Then on October 1, 1983, the Westchester County Department of Parks, Recreation and Conservation officially reopened the lighthouse to the public one hundred years after the beacon was originally lit.

The seventh lighthouse on the Hudson River is known as The Little Red Lighthouse or Jeffreys Hook Lighthouse built in 1920. The lighthouse is currently located in Fort Washington Park (near 181st Street and the George Washington Bridge) and is open regularly for tours. The lighthouse's original role was to guide the navigation of shipping up the Hudson, the main transportation artery between New York City and the interior parts of Albany, Troy and beyond.

When the George Washington Bridge was erected during the 1930s, it was determined that the lighthouse was no longer needed. Hence, in 1947, it was deactivated and scheduled for demolition. However, a children's book titled, "The Little Red

Lighthouse and the Great Grey Bridge" (written by Hildegard H. Swift), helped save the lighthouse and it then became a popular place in America. Millions of children who loved "The Little Red Lighthouse" spoke out and saved its destruction. Then shortly after they spoke, the Jeffreys Hook Lighthouse was deeded to New York City.

In addition to lighthouses, the estates of the Hudson also represent a long, rich history. Many estates in the mid-Hudson region are connected with various branches of the Livingston family, whose members included politicians, war heroes and one of the five authors of the Declaration of Independence.

At the turn of the last century, the Mills and Vanderbilt families were at the center of New York society life as their estates were redolent with the opulence of American Renaissance. The Hudson Valley's lush landscapes attracted artists to its beauty, inspiring the Hudson River School of Painting.

The estates in the Valley areas varied as the people who constructed them. From Lyndhurst's Gothic castle to Clermont's Federal austerity, popular trends in American living over the course of our history are represented here. Exquisite gardening and landscaping, architecture in a diversity of styles, and fine collections of furnishings, artwork, historical archives, textiles, china and other treasures are maintained in their period condition. The residences are replete with personal possessions and familial details that convey a sense of home, a memory of having been lived in and a deeper understanding for the people who lived there. Sometimes it feels like as though the family has just stepped out for a stroll, giving the visitor time to look around the house before they return.

Today, several organizations oversee the estates of the Hudson Valley, providing the detailed attention and dedication to preservation that allows these unique estates to flourish in modern times. One nonprofit group founded by John D. Rockefeller, Historic Hudson Valley, manages the Sleepy Hollow region estates of Kykuit, Sunnyside, Van Cortlandt Manor as well as the Montgomery Place estate in Annandale-On-Hudson and other historic sites in the lower Hudson Valley. The New York State's Office of Parks, recreation and Historic Preservation maintains Olana, Clermont, and Mills Mansion. Estates such as Locust grove,

Val-Kill, Springwood and Lindenwald are supported as National Historic Landmarks. Other mansions are managed by National Trust Historic Sites or are maintained privately.

In the paragraphs that follow this sentence, you will get a brief, general overview of 16 estates in the Hudson River Valley. First, I will mention the Boscobel Estate, which was built in Crugers, New York in 1804 by States Morris Dyckman, a British Loyalist who returned to the area after the Revolutionary War ended. Today, the mansion is located in Garrison, New York. The house is filled with a large collection of American Federal period antiques and art and its grounds include a rose garden. Every year, many special events are held at Boscobel, including the Hudson Valley Shakespeare Festival held every summer on the front lawn of the estate.

Clermont, is an estate located in Germantown, NY. Clermont has been occupied by seven generations of the influential and affluent Livingston family which included Robert R. Livingston Jr. who was one of the five men who authored the Declaration of Independence and swore George Washington as America's first president.

Livingston's first mansion, a brick Georgian, was burned down by British troops advancing up the Hudson in 1775. The house was rebuilt soon after that and remodeled in the 1920s to the Colonial Revival that stands today. The home's interior depicts the intact belongings of the Livingston family including sculptures from near and abroad and a collection of portraits. Special events hosted at the home include the Heritage Blues Festival, antique shows and croquet tournaments on the lawns.

Another estate along the Hudson Valley is Glenview, which today is located in Yonkers, NY. Glenview was completely built in 1877 and is the restored Victorian mansion. This estate is recognized as one of the best examples of Eastlake interior styling, including extensive woodwork and stenciling inspired by motifs of nature. So far, four rooms in the Glenview residence have been restored to their turn of the century condition, which includes the magnificently tiled Great Hall.

Glenview visitors can see the five galleries of exhibits in the Hudson River Museum and there are regularly scheduled events held at the Andrus Planetarium.

Today, if you are headed to the Sleepy Hollow (Tarrytown, part of Westchester County, NY) area (famous for the Headless Horseman tale), you can see the furnished granite-made Kykuit house, which is one of the Rockefeller family homes, and a Georgian mansion that towers above series of stone terraces and formal gardens. The beaux-arts landscape is home to Governor Nelson Rockefeller's impressive collection of 20th century sculpture, which includes works by Noguchi, Calder and Picasso. A variety of tours of the gardens and sculpture are offered to the public to highlight the collection. Moreover, visitors can see a Coach barn, which showcases Rockefeller's horse-drawn carriages and antique automobiles. Kykuit tours commence at Phillipsburg Manor or sightseers can take the ferry to Kykuit by calling NY Waterways at 1-800-53-FERRY.

The Lindenwald Estate sits in Kinderhook, NY. Martin Van Buren, the eighth president of the United States, was born in Lindenwald and then retired there after he left the oval office. In 1839, Van Buren bought the existing estate and then quickly had it remodeled from the "old fashioned" Federal style to the popular Italianate revival style. The home and furnishings were restored to its Italianate condition when Van Buren resided there. The Lindenwald mansion hosts an extensive, huge museum collection, which includes furnishings, textiles and a large collection of historic wallpaper. Several archeological sites on the property have made artifacts, which are presently on display.

Another estate of interest to many is the Mills Mansion located in Staatsburg, NY. Mills Mansion was erected around 1895 and the 65-room Autumn Residence of the Mills family (once the center of New York society) displays Beaux Arts neoclassical styling and elaborate English and French furnishings. The inside of the Mills estate boasts lavish furnishings, mostly in the 17th and 18th century French style, combined with artifacts and paintings which reflect the family's deep pride in its American heritage. Public tours of the Mills mansion are conducted from April through October.

In addition to mansions, famous parks are located on the Hudson Valley. One park well known to New York residents and many tourists is Bear Mountain State Park. Bear Mountain State Park in Bear Mountain, NY has something for everyone. From miles of hiking trails to an inn, the park offers nature in all of its glory and beauty for a family just out for a scenic Sunday stroll to the avid outdoorsman. Bear Mountain is open 365 days a year from 8 a.m. to dusk. The swimming pool is open from Memorial Day to Labor Day and the outdoor ice rink is open from November through March. Visitors can also rent rowboats and paddle boats, playgrounds and picnic areas are located throughout the park and different craft shows and festivals are held throughout the year. Bear Mountain Park also has a zoo where visitors can glance at many of the animals which live in the area, such as deer, bobcat, hawk, turkey, bald eagle, river otter, fox, black bear and different kinds of fish.

Nestled along the Hudson River, the name, Bear Mountain, was derived due to the profile of the mountain resembling a bear lying down. The park is located about 50 miles north of New York City at the intersection of the Palisades Parkway and Route 9W. Rail commuters can take the Metro-North Railroad to the Peekskill or Garrison stations and take a taxi across the river to the park. Visitors can also travel round-trip to Bear Mountain and the U.S. Military Academy at West Point on the Hudson River Dayliner. The ship originates from Pier 81 at the end of West 41st Street in New York City and it travels as far north as Poughkeepsie on its nine-hour, 150-mile trip. Passengers can see attractions along the way, which include the George Washington and Tappan Zee Bridges, the Cloisters and the Palisades.

Besides Bear Mountain, another park of interest for residents and tourists is Clermont State Historic Park, a large wooded park on the eastern shore of the river, located on Route 9G in Germantown, NY. The Clermont State Site was the Hudson River seat of New York's politically and socially prominent Livingston family. In fact, Robert Livingston helped draft the Declaration of Independence, swore in George Washington as our first president, and assisted in the development of the steamboat. The grounds also offer trails, gardens and facilities for winter sports. Once you are at Clermont State Historic Park, you can also enjoy scenic views of the Hudson River and Catskill Mountains.

Another attraction along the Hudson is in Kingston, New York (about 50 miles south of Albany, NY), home to Kingston Point Beach. Kingston Point Beach features a bathing beach on the

Hudson, a playground, picnic area and boat launch. In addition, this municipal beach provides facilities for picnicking, boating, windsurfing and even swimming on the shores of the Hudson River.

Other parks by the Hudson to visit are located in the river towns of Westchester County, NY. In Peekskill, at a park in the Riverfront Green near Route 9, visitors can sit on a riverside bench, fly a kite, enjoy a picnic and children can enjoy a playground. The park also has a public boat-launching ramp available for boaters and fishermen. In addition, many concerts and special events are held there throughout the year. Just south of Peekskill's Riverfront Park is Charles Point Pier Park that offers stunning views of the Hudson River. Fishing is also allowed in this area with a valid license. Another park, Blue Mountain Reservation, is a 1,888-acre park that offers guests an array of picnic areas, hiking trails, playground facilities, a small lake, fishing and a beach. One wooded trail offers a climb to the top of Mount Spitzenburg for a spectacular view of the Hudson Valley clear to New York City.

In Cortlandt, NY, you can visit six popular parks. One is the Old Croton Aqueduct Trailway, a state-owned, 16-mile trailway that offers pedestrians a scenic walk from northern Westchester County into New York City, or vice versa, following the path of the aqueduct that was once used to bring fresh water from the Croton River to the city. Although the trailway is mostly a walking path, it does have some sections suitable for horseback riding. The trail starts on the south side of the Croton Dam and along the way, walkers can see old ventilator shafts and a weir chamber, used to spill off wastewater during floods. As the trail goes through Tarrytown and North Tarrytown it passes right through Sleepy Hollow country, passing behind the Old Dutch Church cemetery made famous in Washington Irving's stories and crossing the Pocantico River near the spot where the Headless Horseman scared Ichabod Crane. In addition, many parts of the trail offer magnificent views of the Hudson River. A second Croton-based park is the Croton Gorge Park located by the Croton Dam. The dam in Croton gives visitors a great view as water cascades first down a tiered hill and then into the rocky Croton River. This gorge park is also an ideal location for fishing as well as picnicking with the family. A playground area for kids and ball fields are also available. Furthermore, the Croton Aqueduct Trail takes hikers on a scenic journey through the woods and if they walk far enough (about 2 1/2 miles), they will get a good view of the Hudson River. During the winter, this area is a great place for sledding and cross-country skiing.

Other parks in the Cortlandt area include George's Island Park, Sportsman Center and Sprout Brook Park. George's Island Park, located in Montrose, NY, is a beautiful park on the shore of the Hudson River and is a well-known area for boat launching. This site can accommodate boats up to 21 feet and is open seven days a week from April through October. Ball fields are in the park and it offers hiking, fishing, picnicking and nature study. Another park, the Sportsman Center, which is located on 300 acres of the Blue Mountain Reservation, provides convenient and safe areas for small bore and large bore rifle, pistol and archery. New York State pistol permit required for pistols only. This park is open Saturdays, Sundays and holidays. During April to November, Thursday and Friday hours are offered. Finally, Cortlandt's Sprout Brook Park, a popular summer destination for locales, is a place where guests can enjoy riding on a 300-foot waterslide, a game of horseshoes or a family picnic. All sliders must be at least 48 inches tall. The park is open to the public but admission fees are higher for non-residents of Cortlandt Township. It is open weekends in June, daily through Labor Day once school is out for the year.

Other Hudson River Parks can be seen in Croton-on-Hudson where you will find Croton Point Park and in Ossining, home to Teatown Lake Reservation and Briarcliff-Peekskill Trailway. Croton Point Park offers cabin, tent and trailer camping May through October and has a beach on the Hudson River. The beach is open daily from June through Labor Day. In addition, children's play areas, softball fields, picnicking, fishing and hiking are offered to the public. Many special events and outdoor concerts are held here and the park is within walking distance from the Croton-Harmon railroad station. Ossining is where you can stop by Teatown Lake Reservation, a nature preserve and education center, which offers special classes and programs to anyone who is interested. Park naturalists give presentations, featuring live animals, birds of prey, reptiles, bees and much more. Hiking trails also roam the hilly terrain, wetlands and hardwood forest. The facility also features indoor exhibits and a nature store. As for the Briarcliff-Peekskill Trailway, a 12-mile hiking trail that runs between Route 9A in Ossining and the Blue Mountain Reservation in Peekskill, it offers great views of the Hudson River from the peak of Mount Spitzenburg.

Sleepy Hollow is another Hudson River town, which features two popular parks, Rockefeller State Preserve and Kingsland Point Park. Rockefeller State Preserve features meadows, woodlands, wetlands and a 24-acre lake. People also go there to jog, cross-country ski or study nature. Fishing licenses are required and horseback riding is allowed with a permit. Kykuit, former home of the Rockefellers and one of the valley's most popular attractions, is located next to the preserve and tours of the historic home leave from Philipsburg Manor. A second well-known attraction in Sleepy Hollow is Kingsland Point Park. This place is a scenic county park located right on the Hudson River. This is where people take a walk along the river and enjoy a picnic. It is open during the season to Westchester County residents only.

Travel on North Broadway (Route 9) to Tarrytown, NY and you can visit Patriot's Park. This is a passive park where you can explore some history by viewing the statue commemorating the patriots who captured Major John Andre. Andre was the British officer seized as he made his way through what is now Tarrytown with the plans for West Point, given to him by Benedict Arnold. Guests can also enjoy lunch on a park bench and children can play at a playground. A second Tarrytown park open to the public is the popular Pierson Park on West Main Street. Visitors can get good views of the Hudson River and Palisades as they walk, fish, have a barbecue, picnic or play tennis and basketball.

Moving south on the Hudson River Line we come to Yonkers, a large city in Westchester County. Once in Yonkers, the public can visit two riverfront parks and a preserve. One park, Tibbetts Brook Park on Midland Ave., offers people hiking, swimming, picnicking, and fishing. During the winter, skiing, sledding and ice-skating are among the activities people can enjoy here. Westchester County park passes are required for admission. A second riverside park in Yonkers is Sprain Ridge Park on Jackson Ave. This 270-acre park in the county's southern end features three swimming pools and two picnic areas. The park also has many ravines, ponds and three hiking trails with views overlooking the Sprain Ridge Reservoir. The Sprain Brook Parkway on the East and the Gov. Thomas E. Dewey Thruway on the West border the reservoir's wooded area (about a half a mile wide and three miles long). A county park pass is required for admission. Yonkers is also home to the Lenoir Preserve on Dudley Street. This is a 40-acre preserve featuring a rolling lawn and obstructed views of the Hudson River. A nature center staffed with a naturalist and programs offered each weekend make this a great place to bring the family. Group tours are available by reservation. The preserve is open Wednesday through Sunday, from 9 a.m. to 5 p.m.

As you head further south on the Hudson River Line you will come across another park, the Hudson River Park, by the Hudson River and New York Harbor. Hudson River Park begins at Battery Place with a walkway and bikeway that continues along the entire length of the park to 59th Street. From there, it connects the Riverside South Park and Riverside Park. This area marks the beginning of the Hudson River Valley Greenway Trail that will eventually run all the way to Troy, north of Albany, NY. Today, the 550-acre park includes 400 acres of open water that provides an exciting public venue for touring, boating, fishing, swimming and many other activities.

The heart of the park features 13 old maritime piers, which were reconstructed as public park spaces. The piers include lawns and gardens, scenic overlooks, picnic areas, ball fields, a dog run, children's playground, a basketball court, a living museum, historic boats, volleyball courts, and other attractions. In addition, the park has a waterfront esplanade running the length of the park that gives visitors great views of the Hudson. Adjacent to the grassy stretch along the shore, there are four miles of gardens, places to rent bikes, fountains, and tennis courts.

Many people enjoy parks on the banks of the Hudson where they can play, relax and view the water. Yet besides parks, the public can also visit agriculture areas, gardens, and wineries along the Hudson. From the Adirondacks to New York City, the Hudson flows past nearly one million acres of farmland. The Hudson River ecosystem provides the ideal climate for fruit farmers to grow apples, peaches, pears, plums, pumpkins, nectarines, apricots, raspberries, blueberries, strawberries, cherries, melons, tomatoes and grapes. The Hudson Valley is also home to the unique "black dirt" region of Orange County, an area of highly productive soils for growing onions, lettuce and other vegetables. Vegetables typically harvested within the Hudson Valley are beets, carrots, mushrooms, potatoes, sprout, asparagus and zucchini. In addition, many concentrations of sweet corn are found in the Lower Hudson Valley.

The Hudson Valley is also an ideal location for visitors to see and enjoy the beauty of gardens. Two popular gardens are located at New York's Montgomery Place and Lasdon Park. Once you visit Montgomery Place at Annandale-on-Hudson, you will see beautiful, formal gardens, in a Colonial-Revival pattern, mixed with herbs and flowers. This garden blooms with yarrow, curly chive, rosemary, lemon balm and catmint plants. And along one border of the garden, you will see hot colors of floral palette (bright yellows, purples & reds) along with other light and airy flowers (blues, pinks & whites). Another area in Montgomery features its rough garden, which is divided by a waterfall and a stream. That's where plants, such as pink rhododendron, white elderberry and blue lacecap hydrangea, grow in a variety of ways and you will also hear frogs splashing in the water. Montgomery Place is open on weekends May to October, from 10 a.m. to 5 p.m. and admission is $5.

Lasdon Park in Somers, NY, is where you will see an elegant, formal garden. Pots of plants with flowers are changed in the garden three times a year. In the summer, the garden is full of deep whites, reds and purples, with nicotiana, petunias and alyssum among the flowers. Also during the summer months, coneflowers of all colors (white, pink, red, orange, etc.) dominate the park's other gardens. In the spring, azaleas bloom on a nearby hill at the park and they form a rainbow that includes magenta, lavender, coral, white and hot pink flowers. The park is open daily year-round, from 8 a.m. to 4 p.m. and admission is free.

Just like you'll find farmland and lush gardens north of New York City, travel up the Hudson River Line and you will come across one of America's most historic wine regions. Today, the Hudson River Region hosts more than 20 wineries (the landscape thrives in harvesting apples, grapes & other fruit) as the area builds on the tradition of the oldest vineyard and winery in the United States. A pioneering region for French-American grape varieties such as Baco Noir and Seyval Blanc, the Hudson River Region has proved hospitable to the more delicate European grape varieties such as Cabernet Franc and Chardonnay.

Within the larger Hudson River Region, there are 21 wineries on the west side of the river that have organized a "Shawangunk Wine Trail" in New Paltz, NY named after a nearby mountain range. Some of New York State's western wineries include the New York Harvest Cellars, Inc. in Glens Falls, Applewood Winery in Warwick, Brotherhood America's oldest Winery, Ltd. in Washingtonville, Pazdar Winery in Scotchtown and Mountain View Winery, LLC in Cambridge. The Shawangunk Wine Trail publishes a special brochure and hosts special events during the year.

On the eastern side of the river, you will find 9 more wineries. The river's east end is where you will find the Dutchess Wine Trail in Clinton Comers, NY. Some of the river's western wineries include the New York Harvest Cellars in Granville, Alison Wines & Vineyards in Red Hook, North Salem Vineyard, Inc. in North Salem, Prospero Winery in Pleasantville and the Cascade Mountain Winery & Restaurant in Amenia. Like the Shawangunk Wine Trail, the Dutchess Wine Trail welcomes visitors as well.

In addition to attractions, the Hudson River offers visitors and residents many opportunities to engage in recreational activities. For example, one popular activity is recreational fishing.

First and foremost, the public needs to understand that recreational fishing in the Hudson is crucial to the management of fish in the river's estuary. Based on aerial angler counts, the Hudson estuary recreational fishery is among the fastest growing fisheries in New York State. Information on use patterns and angler harvest are important to evaluate the status of anadromous and resident fish stocks, impacts of management actions and the economic value of recreational use. The popularity of the black bass and striped bass fishery has led to an increase in recreational fishing for all Hudson River species.

Each year, riverbank anglers and fishermen on boats come to the Hudson hoping to catch a good number of fish. The fishing season in the Hudson runs from March 16 to November 30 and people can fish anywhere on the river above the George Washington Bridge. In fact, there are even nine New York State-designated fishing spots along the Metro-North line (on the river's East Side) where anglers now go to fish by the train tracks. These locations include Greystone station in Yonkers (Westchester County), Riverdale station in the Bronx (Bronx County), Sparta Dock in Ossining and Annsville Creek in Cortlandt (both in Westchester County) and Arden Point and Little Stony Point in Philipstown (both in Putnam County). In addition, there's Cold Spring station (Putnam County), Dennings Point in Beacon and Beacon riverfront (both in Dutchess County). Moreover, to make it easy for anglers, no fishing license is required on the Hudson up to Troy Dam. However, you will need a license to fish tributaries leading into the river.

The Hudson now has enjoyed a water-quality comeback and resurgence in top-rate angling that also makes it a prime region in the northeastern U.S. to fish for largemouth and smallmouth bass. It is also a good spring spot for stripers (striped bass). Ideal striper fishing areas include Croton Point, Storm King Mountain, Denning Point, Esopus Meadows and the vicinity of Rondout, Esopus, and Catskill Creeks. For many years, striped bass has been a favorite treat for anglers. However, fishermen do have to be aware of limits. The limits for fishermen are that they can keep any fish 18 inches or larger, smaller fish must be returned and the daily limit is one fish per person. Bait which anglers commonly use to catch striped bass includes bloodworms, sandworms, and chunks of herring, chunks of bunker and eels. Lures used are striper swipers, bombers and rapalas. The popularity of fishing for striped bass in the Hudson has increased tremendously and many people are surprised that these fish weigh up to 50 pounds. Of course the sizes do differ, but it's not uncommon to catch striped bass in the 20-25 pound range on a regular basis during the season. During the summer, in addition to bass, anglers can catch many adult bluefish (marine species) that are found in the saline parts of the lower river. These "alligator blues," named for their strong jaws and teeth, can also weigh up to 19 pounds. Besides bluefish, some of the best waters to fish for carp are in the Hudson River. Anglers fishing for carp often make doughballs to use as bait and sometimes use whole kernel corn for bait in designated areas.

Many fishermen along the Hudson River enjoy shoreline fishing. However, other anglers like to fish from a boat. The Hudson River has a lot of boat launch ramps in New York and a few in New Jersey for both anglers and boaters.

In New York City, fishermen with boats can head to the Dyckman Marina Ramp. The ramp is located at the northern end of Manhattan and the marina is at the western end of Dyckman Street. There is parking for about 25 cars with trailers and boats up to 28 feet long are permitted. However, boaters must beware that the ramp is in the main channel of the Hudson with no break from the numerous wakes, currents and winds.

North of the New York Harbor is where anglers will find Yonkers Municipal Boat Ramp located at the northern end of Kennedy Marina Park. This ramp is a double width ramp enabling two boats to be launched at the same time. The ramp has parking available for 50 cars with trailers. Use of the ramp is limited to the launching and pulling of vessels only and it's a good place to launch for fishing the Tappan Zee Bridge and Croton area.

Like Yonkers, Tarrytown has a ramp named the Washington Irving Boat Club. This ramp is located on the south end of the boat club and is doublewide for launching two boats at a time. There is limited maneuvering room at the top of the ramp with buildings only forty feet away. As for parking, boaters can park in the municipal lot just north of the boat club available only on weekends.

On the west shore of the Hudson in Nyack, anglers can bring their vessels to the Nyack Municipal Boat Launch Ramp where there is ample room to maneuver one's car and trailer. Parking is limited to 50 cars with trailers and hours of operation are from dawn to dusk.

Fishermen traveling to the town of Ossining can go to the Ossining Municipal Launch Ramp. This ramp is made of smooth concrete where boaters can launch one boat at a time from it. Launching vessels over 26 feet is not allowed. Operation hours start on May 1st and end on September 30th. This ramp is very difficult at low tide and some boats will have to wait for tidal changes. This can be inconvenient for a couple of hours during full moon and new tides. Ossining officials advise boaters not to launch or recover their boats at low tide.

In Croton-on-the-Hudson, fisherman with boats can go to the Senasqua Park Launch Ramp, which is a singlewide concrete ramp with a sharp drop off at the water line. The ramp becomes difficult at low tides, as does many ramps along the Hudson, specifically with bigger boats (over 22 feet long). Hours of operation are from 8 a.m. to 8 p.m. from the end of April to October.

Another ramp, located on the north end of the Haverstraw Marina, is located in West Haverstraw. This ramp is concrete, double width, but only the left-hand side is useable. The ramp is out of the main currents of the river and there are floating docks on the left side. Fortunately, low tidal conditions are not an issue at this facility. There is a lot of maneuvering room and parking for about 50 cars with trailers. You can also make arrangements to keep your boat in the water overnight at this ramp and there is good fishing just across the Haverstraw Bay. In addition, anglers can access a tackle store at the marina. The hours of operation are from 8 a.m. to 8 p.m. and by appointment.

In Stony Point, you will find the Belle Harbor Marina. The ramp in this marina is made of single-width smooth concrete and contains a 50-foot floating dock on its north side. The ramp is lit at night and is located in a quiet cove, out of currents and wakes of the main river. Parking is available for over 50 car/trailer combinations and the hours of operation are flexible.

A second marina located in Stony Point is the Stony Point Bay Marina and Yacht Club. The ramp in this marina is a single-width concrete ramp that is equipped with a twenty-foot floating dock on the north side and on the south side, it has a fifty-foot floating dock. This ramp feeds into a cove in the marina and is protected from the currents and wakes of the main river channel. Low tide is not a big concern for this ramp. In addition, there is unlimited maneuvering room with parking for more than 50 cars with trailers.

Then there's Montrose, NY, home to the Georges Island Park Launch Ramp. The ramp at Georges Island is capable of launching four boats at a time with two floating docks. The center ramp is doublewide and will easily handle two boats. The ramps are constructed with asphalt and concrete with limited maneuvering room for cars with trailers. Parking is available for about 100 cars with trailers and the park has picnic tables, grills, a playground and hiking trails. Vessels up to 21 feet are allowed and operation hours are from 8 a.m. to dusk from April to October.

Peekskill also features a ramp; it's called the Peekskill Municipal Launch Ramp. The Peekskill Ramp is doublewide for launching two vessels at a time and is equipped with a fifty-foot floating dock down the center. The west ramp is made of concrete while the east ramp is comprised of asphalt. Each ramp has a different pitch to it so boaters must try each ramp to determine which one is best for them during each tide.

The ramp in Peekskill has enough parking for fifty cars with trailers. Moreover, restaurants and stores are within walking distance of the ramps. In addition, the facility has picnic tables and restrooms. Operation hours are from 8 a.m. to 10 p.m.

The West Shore of the Hudson is where fishermen with boats will find the Newburgh Municipal Launch Ramp. This ramp is large enough for four vessels to launch at the same time. There is also unlimited room for boat launching and parking available for about 25 cars with trailers.

The Newburgh Ramp is a very popular ramp with many anglers not moving more than several hundred yards from the ramp to fish. In April, it's common to see fifty boats drifting in front of this ramp and you will notice many hooked striped bass on these vessels.

For fishermen in the New Hamburg, NY area, there's White's Hudson River Marina. The ramp in New Hamburg is a singlewide concrete launch that feeds directly into the marina. The ramp has a 50-foot floating dock and at low tide, the ramp can hold two feet of water. There is also unlimited maneuvering room for cars and trailers. The marina is a full service facility that offers boaters gas, goods, and other services. The ramp's operation hours are flexible.

In Poughkeepsie, anglers will find the Poughkeepsie Municipal Launch Ramp. This is a public doublewide ramp made of concrete that feeds into the main channel of the river. It also has unlimited maneuvering for cars and trailers where parking is available for about thirty of these vehicles. In addition, the Poughkeepsie Ramp offers visitors picnic tables, barbecues and a restaurant. Hours of operation are from 8 a.m. to 9 p.m.

Another ramp on the East Shore of the Hudson is called Andros River Road Marina located in Hyde Park. The ramp is a singlewide, concrete and asphalt complex that feeds into a protected cove into the marina. However, boaters must beware those vessels over 3 feet 6 inches will not be able to clear the railroad bridge separating the cove from the river.

Fortunately, the ramp can hold 30 car and trailer combinations and there is unlimited maneuvering room for these vehicles. There is also a picnic area on the property and operation hours are flexible.

In addition to boat ramps that fishermen can visit in New York, there are some ramps they can access in New Jersey. In New Jersey, three popular ramps are located in Jersey City, Fort Lee and Englewood Cliffs.

In Jersey City, on the West Shore of the Hudson, anglers will see Liberty State Park Launch Ramp. The ramp is doublewide and equipped with a fixed dock down the middle. It also features a 56-foot floating dock at the south end of the ramp so fishermen can tie up their boats. The ramp is made of concrete and is located in a sheltered cove that is out of the main winds, wakes, and currents of the Hudson River. The ramp is also wide open for maneuvering and has parking for more than 100 cars with trailers. Operation hours are from 6 a.m. to 10 p.m. from the beginning of April until the end of October.

North of Jersey City in Fort Lee is where boaters will see Hazzard's Launch Ramp. Located under the George Washington Bridge inside Palisades Interstate Park, this ramp features a doublewide, two boat-launching, concrete area with an eighty-foot floating dock down the center. The lights from the GW Bridge illuminate the whole ramp during nighttime and parking is available for fifty cars with trailers. Operation hours are from 8 a.m. until dusk, from the beginning of April until the end of October.

The Hazzard's Launch Ramp has a 24-foot maximum length for boats and is in the main current of the river and wakes. Boaters must also deal with currents and wind when they launch vessels from this site. But despite the pitfalls, a new breakwater was built on the south side of the ramp to help boaters in that situation.

Travel to the West Shore of the Hudson and boaters will find the Englewood Boat Basin in Englewood Cliffs, NJ. This boat ramp is located on a sandy beach area and is geared strictly towards car-topped, non-trailered boats. Trailered boats are not allowed at this site. However, a playground, picnic tables, hiking trails and nature trails are on the premises. Operation hours are from 8 a.m. until dark.

In addition to fish, fishing and boat ramps, there's shellfish, specifically blue crabs, found in the Hudson, which are also important to both commercial and recreational fishermen. Most commercial activity takes place between Piermont and Poughkeepsie but state officials have documented the presence of blue crabs in the tidal estuary from New York Harbor to Troy. Although blue crabs will be found throughout the whole estuary, the closer to sea you go the larger they will be. In the Tappan Zee and Haverstraw Bay areas, blue crabs can grow to 9 inches across their carapace. Recreational crabbers often run a series of baited traps (square, wire mesh boxes with doors that snap shut upon retrieval) from shore or from a small boat. Some people work from shore with a hand line and long-handled net; tie the bait (Atlantic menhaden & chicken necks are common crab baits in the Hudson) to a length of twine, toss into the river and allow to sink; after an interval retrieve slowly into the range of the hand net. Blue crabs are aggressive predators and will usually hang onto the bait until within reach. Crabs are active from June through October.

Besides fishing and crabbing, people of all ages can enjoy other water activities. Regardless of one's ability level, he or she can rent a canoe or kayak for a day or a week on the lower Hudson River Gorge and get professional lessons and safety instructions. In fact, the Hudson River today is one of the major canoeing and kayaking spots in the northeast United States. The Hudson is easier to navigate in a kayak than a canoe and the number of kayakers running the gorge has steadily increased. The river offers kayakers constant changes of scenery and the finest exposure to serene hamlets, woodlands and wildlife. The Hudson is a tidal estuary (the water flows with the tides, not in any stable direction), which means the current is never swift and its width adds to the overall experience of solitary viewing its surroundings.

The Hudson River and its tributaries are located in scenic places and are best explored and found by kayak. Within the past few years, paddle sports have become more popular and a huge desire to enjoy the Hudson Valley's outdoor activities means that many more people are using kayaks to navigate and explore the Hudson River. If anyone is going to paddle on the Hudson his or her experience depends on making the correct choices. The paddleboat one chooses, the skills he or she possesses, and his or her knowledge of the aquatic environment are the main factors to a safe and fun kayaking experience.

To enjoy the Hudson safely by kayak means that a person needs the right boat. To paddle safely on the river means that you need a sea kayak. Sea kayaks handle the conditions of an ocean environment and are perfect for navigating the Hudson. The recommended Hudson River kayak is sixteen feet or longer with two bulkheads (a bulkhead is an interior wall that seals off one or both ends of the boat making it watertight so if the vessel capsizes it will not sink).

Kayakers also need to be aware that the water level of the Hudson River rises and drops about four feet every six hours. These fluctuations in the river level occur from Manhattan all the way north to Troy, where it is dammed. With this Ebb (water going out of the river) and Flood (water coming into the river) of the tide happening around the clock, the Hudson River's current and water level is always changing and the kayaker needs to know this. At one point in the day you may have enough water to paddle on a specific portion of the river, then a few hours later when the tide goes out you may be stuck in the mud. Moreover, it is also more difficult to paddle on the river against the current.

Also before you paddle, check the conditions in and near the river. Three conditions that can change at any time are weather, wind and waves. You must know these variables and plan your day of kayaking around them. In addition, always remember that you should never paddle if there is lightning, thunder or even if thunder or lightning is forecast. Your worst enemy can also be wind so for the inexperienced paddler it is wise to remain off the water if the forecast is for winds higher than 10 mph.

Besides wind, there are waves. Waves on the river generally come form two sources, the wind and boat traffic. Wind waves get bigger and harder to paddle in when the wind speed increases and the length of fetch (word refers to the distance over which wind travels without encountering obstructions) increases. The rule is the longer the fetch, the more powerful the waves. Boats under motor of any size make a wave or wake. Depending on the size of the vessel and how far you are from it, boat wake can capsize you if you are a new paddler. Always look out for waves if you encounter boat traffic.

Rules of the river apply to every vessel including paddlers on kayaks or canoes. One of the most current dangers to the kayaker on the Hudson River is the commercial shipping traffic. The international shipping lane begins at New York City and stretches all the way to the Port of Albany. You will see barges and tugs, tankers, container ships, passenger vessels, ferries, yachts, fishing boats, sail boats and jet skis on any day maneuvering on the Hudson. Obviously all of these vessels are much larger than a kayak so if you want to return from your paddling trip in one piece, you need to remember the unwritten Rule of Tonnage. Simply put, if the vessel is bigger than you, get out of its way. Paddlers also need to be aware of where the shipping channel is and how it is marked. Carrying a nautical chart (map) is a good idea and when you see it you will see that the shipping channel is clearly marked with green and red buoys (cans & nuns). The safest place for the novice kayaker to paddle is well outside the shipping lane.

Furthermore, paddlers need to go over a checklist before they go on the river. This checklist includes wearing a properly fitted lifejacket at all times; being comfortable in the water (learn how to swim); and file a float plan (where and when you are leaving, where and when you are returning, file this with friends, families or the authorities). The list also consists of dressing for immersion in the water (wet suits, dry suits, etc.); wear appropriate footwear and clothing (no cotton); and check your boat's flotation before you leave. You must also paddle with a group, know how to save yourself and others if there's a capsize, paddle within your skill level, follow all local, state and federal laws, and take a lesson.

Besides kayakers, those beginners who choose to navigate the Hudson on a sailboat must be aware of the river's potential dangers that include its strong currents, dense commercial traffic, and the lack of buoys limit. Sailboat students must also learn charts and navigation rules pertaining to the Hudson River.

In addition to kayakers and others knowing the rules of the river, each summer the annual Great Hudson River Paddle (GHRP) is organized on the Hudson River. The GHRP is an event geared for every type of paddler regardless of his or her experience or skill level.

GHRP is held each year to celebrate the 156-mile-long Hudson River Greenway Water Trail (HRGWT), the improvement of public access to the Hudson River, and the heritage and diversity of the Hudson River Valley's riverside communities. Every summer, a group of up to thirty paddlers and their guides will begin their trip from Albany to New York City, camping at prearranged destinations along the way. In addition, public festivals will be held near many stopover points to celebrate the Hudson River Valley's communities and the Greenway Water Trail.

When it comes to paddlers, there are many parts of the Hudson River that are popular among kayakers for natural beauty and scenery. For instance, paddling in the area near Sleepy Hollow is great for seeing the gradual change-taking place upon the river from being lined with pollution-spewing factories to expansive parks and greenery. On Pollopel Island, north of Cold Springs, kayakers can see the haunting Bannerman Castle. Then when you paddle just north of Poughkeepsie, you can spot Norrie State Park. This park has been named the "Jewel of the Hudson" for its views of nature and of wildlife. Among the birds you can watch there include great blue heron, wild turkeys, water osprey, snow geese, kingfishers, red-tailed hawks and bald eagles.

At Tivoli Bays, on the eastern side of the river, you can catch views of the Catskill Mountains, paddle through marshland and visit the river islands. Waterfowl, such as the kingfisher and swans, are prevalent as well. Meanwhile, on the Hudson's western shore near the town of Catskill, is an area that has been a magnet for poets and artists for almost two centuries and there's an old lighthouse paddlers can see up close near Athens-Hudson, just north of Catskill. The Delaware River, slightly west of the Catskills, is another popular paddling and kayaking route. There are several paddling and kayaking outfitters throughout the Catskills and Hudson Valley region, near both the Hudson River and Delaware River.

The Hudson is also home to white-water rafters. During the spring, nestled in a pristine part of the central Adirondacks, the Hudson River Gorge is ranked as one of the most exciting whitewater runs in America. Rafters can enjoy the blending of wilderness scenery with western-like whitewater. This region marks what the entire Hudson River used to be; that is crystal clear, clean, powerful and alive, as the river's unbridled whitewater thunders along 500-foot granite cliffs. Whitewater rafters can enjoy a fun rush under an array of tall granite cliffs through stretches of the gorge's 17-mile run. The Hudson River's whitewater is most powerful during the spring and fall. Rafting is a little more moderate in the middle of summer. Yet throughout the whole season, scheduled whitewater dam releases assure a good rafting adventure.

From June to October, the upper Hudson becomes a different waterway than the thunderous rush that characterizes the river in April and May. During the summer, the river is family friendly; a waterway which offers people peaceful swimming holes. Some secluded swimming spots for families can be found in the New York counties of Westchester, Rockland and Putnam. Lazy river tubing is another popular summer sport for families and friends. Tubing is a fun water activity that just about anyone can do on the lower Hudson River Gorge. River tubing is done on clean, warm, water with an average depth of 3 feet. It is easy to learn for people of all ages and local tube companies provide riders with life jackets.

In addition to fishing and other water activities, anyone that enjoys walking or hiking should do so along the scenic Hudson River and Ulster County, New York is one good place for them to go. Ulster County is an area where the Catskills meet the Hudson.

Some attractions in the Catskill Mountain area include Barry Knight Guided Walks, Belleayre Mountain, Catskill Mountain Club and Where the Pavement Ends.

Barry Knight Guided Walks in West Hurley, NY is an area where guests can easily hike to the campsite, tower, view the Catskills, Ashokan Reservoir, Mohonk Mountain House and other points of interest. In Highmount, NY, there's Belleayre Mountain that offers hiking in the Catskill Forest Preserve. Elevations range from 600 to 4,200 feet of varied terrain within northern hardwoods. Once you're there, you can hike any ski trail, to the summit, to Pine Hill Lake, or walk in the Belleayre Mountain Interpretive Adventure Trail.

The Catskill Mountain Club in Pine Hill, NY is devoted to outdoor recreation, public land stewardship, education, hiking, camping, fishing, hunting, kayaking, canoeing, biking and nature-related pursuits in the Catskill Mountains. Travel to Stone Ridge, NY and that's where you will find the site of Where the Pavement Ends. That is where you can participate in guided hikes and backpacking trips that are tailored to individual interests and abilities.

In the Ellenville, NY area, there is a walking and hiking spot called Sam's Point Preserve. Sam's Point Preserve is a 5,000-acre preserve situated in the northern Shawangunk Mountains. The preserve contains one of the best examples of ridge-top, dwarf pine barrens in the world. Trails lead to Sam's Point, Verkeerderkill Falls, the Ice Caves, High Point and Indian Rock. The preserve and conservation center is open all year round and the Ice Caves are open seasonally.

In the Kingston, NY area, you will find Lighthouse Park, Perrine's Bridge, Rondout National Historic District Walking Tours and Stockade Historic District Walking Tours.

Lighthouse Park, located in Ulster Park, NY, is a 0.7-acre park that sits directly on the Hudson River. It is open year-round from dawn to dusk and offers stunning views of the Esopus Lighthouse, fishing, and it is accessible by kayak and canoe. In Rifton, NY, there's Perrine's Bridge, which is an antique bridge (the oldest covered bridge) in New York State. The area is open year-round, from dawn to dusk, and has a fishing area.

Kingston-based Rondout National Historic Walking Tours offers visitors a guided tour which traces the rise of Rondout as a rich maritime village with a rich legacy of 19th-century architecture. The Stockade Historical District, also in Kingston, offers the public a guided tour of the neighborhood where New York State was born in 1777 and where many 18th-century, limestone houses still stand. School tours are also available.

Travel to the New Paltz, NY region and you will find over a dozen sites for walking or hiking.

The Black Creek Forest Preserve in Esopus, NY is a 130-acre nature preserve via a 120-foot pedestrian bridge crossing over Black Creek, a tributary of the Hudson River. This preserve also features two miles of trails for walking that lead to the river.

Another preserve in Esopus is the Esopus Meadows Point Preserve and Education Center. The Esopus Meadows is a 100-acre preserve which offers visitors 2 miles of wooden trails across varied terrain with views of Esopus Meadows Lighthouse and the historic Mills Mansion. There are also many opportunities for people to study nature there. In addition, the preserve is connected to Lighthouse Park & Scenic Hudson's Esopus Meadows Environmental Center (operated by Hudson River Sloop Clearwater, Inc.).

In High Falls, NY, you will find Five Locks Walk, a national historic landmark, where you can walk along the towpath of the Delaware and Hudson Canal. This nature spot is open year round from dawn to dusk. In New Paltz, there's the Huguenot Path, which offers guests a self-guided tour through marshlands and around Oxbow Lake. The path of Huguenot sits next to the Historic Huguenot Street and is maintained by the New Paltz Environmental Conservation Commission.

Travelers who go to New Paltz, NY will find The Huguenot Path where they will enjoy a self-guided tour through marshlands and around Oxbow Lake. Huguenot Path is next to the historic Huguenot Street and is maintained by the New Paltz Environmental Conservation Commission. In Ulster Park, there's the John Burroughs Sanctuary, a 192-acre sanctuary that features Greenway trails and a magnificent pond. John Burroughs is open year round and by appointment, guests can get guided tours of the facility.

Another visitors' attraction in New Paltz is the Minnewaska State Park Preserve located in the Shawangunk Mountains. Minnewaska is listed as the "best park" to visit according to the Hudson Valley Magazine. The park is open year round and daily at

9 a.m. Once in the park, guests can participate in swimming, hiking, mountain biking, cross-country skiing, rock climbing and horseback riding. In Gardiner, NY, you will find the Mohonk Preserve Visitors Center. The center (which has rock climbing cliffs) is open daily and features biking, hiking, cross-country skiing, and horseback riding paths.

Travel to Esopus, NY and you will discover Shawangunk Ridge. The ridge is a 570-acre conservation site that offers over 3.5 miles of hiking trails and features woodlands, a wetland bog, interpretive trail, Louisa Pond, and views of the Hudson River and Catskill Mountains. Another park in Esopus is Sleightsburgh Park. This 79-acre park, which is open year round from dawn to dusk, encompasses the south peninsula at the mouth of Rondout Creek (a tributary of the Hudson River), two trails, and a boat launch.

In Wallkill, NY, you will see the Town of Shawangunk Rail Trail. The rail trail represents a 3 plus mile section of rail and trail with views of the Shawangunk Mountain Range. It also provides easy access to both the Wallkill River and the village of Wallkill. A second rail trail, Wallkill Valley Rail Trail, is in New Paltz. This trail offers visitors a 12.2-mile path for walking and bicycling on the rail bed of the old Wallkill Valley Railroad, which used to pass through New Paltz and Gardiner. In addition, the trail passes through scenic countryside, downtown New Paltz and the Huguenot Street area.

Relocating to the Woodstock, NY region, you can see the Overlook Mountain Fire Tower. Overlook Mountain has a 2 1/2-mile trail that gives hikers views of the Hudson Valley, Catskill Mountains, Ashokan Reservoir and the Overlook Hotel ruins.

Moreover, in upstate New York, four more nature sites in the Ulster County area, are open to the public. One in Ulster County is Catskill Forest Preserve, which is state-owned and maintained land within Catskill Park. The preserve has many hiking trails and is made up of 300,000 acres of forests with cliffs, fire towers, meadows, springs, lakes, waterfalls, and wildlife. The second site in Ulster is the D & H Canal Heritage Corridor. D & H Canal offers walkers a 35-mile trail from Kingston to Ellenville, comprised of the Delaware & Hudson Canal tow paths and the Ontario & Western Railway. Throughout the year, visitors can enjoy guided walks, biking, equestrian activities and cross-country skiing. Another Ulster nature attraction is Hudson River Valley Ramble. The Ramble features more than 150 guided walking, hiking, biking, paddling, cultural events and river explorations throughout the 10-county Hudson River National Heritage Area. And finally, another point of interest is the Hudson Valley Rail Trail, a 5-mile nature trail that extends from the Mid-Hudson Bridge in Highland to Route 299. This trail is where people can engage in walking, mountain biking, cross-country skiing and horseback riding. The site also features a 2.5-mile paved portion for rollerblading, wheelchairs, and strollers.

In addition to attractions and recreational sites I already mentioned, Scenic Hudson, Inc. (a New York State-based conservation group) owns, co-owns, and/or manages 28 parks, preserves, and trails along the Hudson throughout the state of New York. Two Scenic Hudson-related parks that I mentioned earlier in this chapter is Lighthouse Park and Black Creek Forest Preserve, both located in Ulster County, NY. Another popular park, which Scenic Hudson fought to preserve, is located at Storm King Mountain in Orange County, NY. This 1,900-acre park is one of the Hudson Valley's most popular landmarks and is the northern gateway to the mythical Hudson Highlands. Besides Storm King Mountain, another park, which is owned by The Scenic Hudson Land Trust, Inc., is Burger Hill Park located in the town of Rhinebeck in Dutchess County, NY. Burger Hill is a very popular hiking, sledding, and picnicking spot that ascends to a 5,550-foot hilltop where visitors can get scenic views of the Hudson River as well as views of the Catskill and Taconic mountains. For more information, visit www.scenichudson.org/tour/parks.htm.

Chapter 5
Newly Completed & Future Hudson Riverfront Development Projects and Hudson River Real Estate Market

From an economic standpoint, development along the Hudson is beneficial for residents, businesses and riverside communities. As long as the Hudson can remain relatively clean, riverfront properties will continue to have a positive impact on New York and New Jersey's local economies, real estate markets, and urban developments.

Regarding positive impact on New York's riverside towns, Ginsburg Development Companies (GDC), a real estate design, development and management company based in Valhalla, NY, recently masterminded a luxury town home enclave project (with scenic river views) that was built at the edge of the Hudson River in Sleepy Hollow, NY.

GDC's Ichabod's Landing, a 3.4-acre site, was one of the first phases of the Westchester RiverWalk, a trail that now runs from Yonkers to Peekskill. Eventually, the RiverWalk is looking to make a 45-mile pedestrian and bicycle path that will run from the Bronx line north to Putnam County. In Peekskill, Ginsburg Properties, a Hawthorne-based developer, recently completed Riverbend, a luxury waterfront complex in which most of its townhomes offer scenic views of the Hudson River.

Peekskill also recently received $8.3 million from the state of New York for its Waterfront Redevelopment Plan. For example, one project the state money is funding is regards to a new Lincoln Plaza on Central Ave. west of Water St. The plaza is now a focal point for the revitalized waterfront area that includes a public gathering square and a "Riverview Walk" pedestrian promenade at Peekskill Landing Park.

Ichabod's Landing, located in Sleepy Hollow and Tarrytown, has a dock and promenade that is accessible by visiting ferries or cruise ships. The Landing also features 44 luxury townhouses with excellent views of the Hudson River, Tappan Zee Bridge and Tarrytown Lighthouse. The buildings have been constructed to give most homeowners scenic views of the Hudson River. Ginsburg Development Companies also built waterfront trails in Sleepy Hollow. Other Ginsburg Development projects include Harbor Square, Hudson Pointe and The Harbors at Haverstraw.

Today, the Ossining Ferry dock and train station area will soon undergo a complete transformation into a mixed-use neighborhood. Ginsburg Development Companies and Capelli Enterprises together will construct One Harbor Square between the existing ferry pier and the Metro North train station, which will help spark a commerce link between the Haverstraw Pier and the Ossining Pier. And once Harbor Square is open on Ossining's riverfront; the community will include 10,000 square feet of restaurant and retail space, 150 condominiums, as well as a waterfront park, water's edge esplanade, kayak launch, fishing pier and a public beach.

Hudson Pointe, a community of 60 luxury townhouses, is now under construction in Poughkeepsie. The town homes range from 1,552 to 2,000 square feet and feature lofts and garden levels as options. Hudson Pointe will be located near a new waterfront park with shops, restaurants, fishing piers and a marina. Located just east of Route 9 on a hill above the Hudson River, Hudson Point offers spectacular views and a lifestyle not duplicated anywhere in Dutchess County.

The Harbors at Haverstraw is a planned riverfront development that will have 850 luxury flats and townhouses served by two clubhouses. The community, which is at the widest point of the Hudson River in New York, will also feature a 12-foot-wide public walkway (with benches), a waterfront park, and waterfront promenade (will run for 1.5 miles along the riverfront). Moreover, the Haverstraw ferry/cruise ships dock recently opened as it accommodated commuters with its newly launched New York Water Taxi service. On September 4, 2007, the New York Water Taxi first set sail from the Haverstraw Ferry Landing. The ferry departed the village of Haverstraw that morning, made one stop in Yonkers, continued on to the World Financial Center, and then to Pier 11 on Wall Street in Lower Manhattan. Furthermore, Ginsburg Development built waterfront trails in Haverstraw.

Another future, giant Ginsburg project consists of the Hudson River Sculpture Trail, which is an ambitious and visionary project for the Hudson River. The developer's goal is to bring a hundred significant outdoor sculptures to the banks of the Hudson

River from Manhattan to Saratoga, NY by September 2009, when the celebration of the Hudson-Fulton-Champlain 400th Anniversary will take place.

In addition to the Ginsburg projects, Scenic Hudson (a Poughkeepsie, NY-based conservation group) has revealed its vision for waterfront development in Yonkers after meeting several times with other organizations, residents, and homeowners who will be affected by planned changes along the city's waterfront. Scenic Hudson's vision features an array of waterfront parks that will provide recreational facilities for children living in downtown Yonkers.

One park set back from the waterfront in Yonkers is Hudson Park, a 266-unit rental property located near the city's historic Main Street Pier. This structure was built off the river's shoreline to make way for a park featuring a walkway and sculpture garden. As part of Scenic Hudson's plan, the organization has offered to partner with the city to acquire funds for creation of more parks along the river. In addition, Scenic Hudson and Yonkers residents proposed having small and mid-scale buildings that provide a mix of uses. The Yonkers waterfront plan proposes that one-third of waterfront development be dedicated to public parkland, making it consistent with development plans in Kingston and Beacon.

In the near future, Yonkers officials also want to open the Hudson River waterfront between the JFK Marina and the Ludlow Train Station, make a river esplanade through the Hepperhan Valley into downtown Yonkers, and restore many of the city's parks. In addition, Yonkers is now working with Westchester County (on a city-county initiative) to eventually open forty-six miles of walkway along the Hudson from Yonkers to Peekskill, NY. The city of Yonkers' part of the city-county riverfront plan would be responsible for a new spray & play park, picnic pavilion, and a boat launch for kayaks and canoes. The Westchester County-financed part of this waterfront plan will include an amphitheater (that will seat up to 350 people) for community events, concerts, and movies.

In Kingston, NY, AVR (a development firm) is proposing to construct a large 1,750-unit housing development on Kingston's Hudson River waterfront, with little room set aside for commercial buildings. Today, the city is reviewing the proposed development and its potential impacts on the environment, the Hudson River, the city of Kingston, and nearby areas. Meanwhile, Hudson River Valley Greenway, a NY-based community organization, is appropriating over $200,000 in the annual state budget to help pay planners to have municipalities create 237 miles of riverside trials, about 50 miles of connector trails, and a 147-mile bike route. Today, the Greenway is encouraging waterfront development specifically in Erie and Niagara counties by trying to convince 13 municipalities on the American side of the Niagara River to make a meaningful change. A plan is now in affect for a 34-mile greenway that would eventually link Lake Ontario to Lake Erie with recreational areas, trails and cultural centers.

In addition to the AVR projects, Scenic Hudson and the city of Beacon plan to redevelop Beacon's waterfront property, which sits just across the Beacon Railroad Station from the museum, as a mixed-use commercial and park project. This plan will enable the station to handle more passengers and bring people directly to the city's waterfront that is walking distance to Scenic Hudson's Long Dock project. This project will include construction of a hotel and a public park.

The Metro-North Railroad is also helping Beacon. The railroad has made improvements to the Beacon Train Station and Metro-North's plans include a three-story parking garage that would be tucked into a hillside. Although the Newburgh-Beacon Ferry provides commuters with a way to get to the Beacon station, Metro-North may also expand its service to the station giving commuters another transportation alternative.

Another town located on the banks of the Hudson River is Newburgh, NY. A developer, Leyland/Alliance LLC, and the city plan to redevelop a vacant 30-acre riverfront site in Newburgh into a mixed-use, pedestrian-oriented neighborhood. The master plan for the city-owned site, which lies on sloping land on the Hudson River waterfront, calls for 511 residential units and several riverside parks. The plan also includes fishing piers, a fish market, plazas, a broadwalk and a tree-lined waterfront promenade.

Leyland's project in Newburgh is part of the city's goals to establish itself as a gateway to the Hudson Valley. Newburgh is about an hour by the Metro-North Commuter Railroad from New York City and has uninterrupted views of the Hudson Valley.

In addition, Troy, NY (another city along the Hudson Line) has undergone waterfront development. The old Mooradian's furniture store on River Street, a 117-year-old building, became home to 48 loft-style or "upscale abodes" residential units. The eight-story brick building, which includes six stories of housing units, is also home to a café and marketplace on the first floor with a terrace overlooking the Hudson River.

In Albany, New York State's capital, the New York State's Department of State of Coastal Resources is now working on improving access to the Corning Preserve, the highlight of which is the Hudson River Way pedestrian bridge over I-787 that directly connects downtown Albany with the Hudson River. The Environmental Protection Fund Local Waterfront Revitalization Program (EPF LWRP) also supports the city as it plans to add a festival space and a promenade to the Corning Preserve.

Waterfront improvements were also made in the village of Waterford in New York State's Capital District, which is located at the confluence of the Hudson and Mohawk Rivers. These improvements were completion of the waterfront promenade, the waterfront visitors center, a boat launch and docks, pocket waterfront parks, beautification of the Hudson River parks on the south and north sides of Broad Street, new commercial development, residential improvements and streetscape improvements.

Hudson riverfront projects are also being funded now in Albany and Schenectady counties. The projects include waterfront improvements along the Hudson River in the town of Bethlehem. Bethlehem is currently developing long-range plans for improving its parks and better connecting its community to the Hudson River. With the help of Scenic Hudson (a New York-based conservation group), the town will soon enlarge an existing riverside park and make designs for a new park a few miles north. A portion of the funding, a matching grant of up to $100,000, will enable Bethlehem to expand Henry Hudson Park (located east of Cedar Hill, NY) at the Hudson River. The rest of Scenic Hudson's funds (a $25,000 matching grant) will be allocated toward designing hiking trails and other amenities on sixty acres of town-owned property.

In addition to waterfront improvements in the regions of Albany, Waterford, and Schenectady, work revitalizing and developing the waterfront area in downtown Buffalo is underway and scheduled for completion by the end of 2009. The first phase of the project focuses on a three-block area near the vacant Buffalo Auditorium and the HSBC Arena. In a later phase, designers want a section of land close to the arena dug out to bring the waterfront up to Main Street. The Buffalo project along the Hudson River costs about $130 million (involves $70 million of private investment) and once finished, housing, shops, and restaurants will be erected on Buffalo's waterfront.

Poughkeepsie is another municipality that has become "waterfront" conscience. A few years ago, the town's Children's Museum opened along the Hudson and that is attracting more families and kids to the river. In addition, the Bonura family, part owners of the Poughkeepsie Grand Hotel on Market Street, has opened the Shadows on the Hudson Restaurant on the southern waterfront.

Yet south of Poughkeepsie and in addition to the city of Yonkers, other Westchester County waterside villages near Yonkers have undergone waterfront revitalization. Some of those communities include Cortlandt, Hastings-on-the-Hudson, Dobbs Ferry, and Irvington.

Cortlandt, unlike other Hudson riverfront communities, is fortunate in that it has many miles and acres of land without railroad tracks along the river. Due to the absence of train tracks in that area, town officials are now willing to purchase these properties for preservation and controlled economic growth reasons.

In fact, now the Town of Cortlandt is negotiating final details to buy eighty waterfront acres that will showcase a sandy river beach suited for swimming as well as a huge quarry lake. The town is also looking at plans for picnic areas, trails, recreation fields, a fishing museum and other passive recreation projects.

Cortlandt has now secured a $350,000 state grant toward the purchase of the land and is looking to secure remaining funds through bonds. Scenic Hudson, a New York State-based organization that works to protect and restore the Hudson River and its landscape, is providing $350,000 in matching support to help the town complete this project.

In Hastings, the long-term vision of the One River Street site represents an opportunity to promote a healthy and sustainable redevelopment to an environmentally damaged property. Today, two important themes of sustainable communities are smart planning and the Green Building design. Both will contribute to a successful redevelopment at the Hastings waterfront.

Smart growth in that new mixed-use development and mixed income housing will focus on its proximity to the railway station and encourage a bicycle friendly design to promote reduced vehicle use.

As for the Green Building design, preserving the historical buildings is important; however, builders must realize how the materials will be used to create the buildings and how the energy and water residents consume to operate them may take a huge toll on the environment (which includes the Hudson River). The One River Street site is full of history, is located at a good waterfront location, and presents a great opportunity for redevelopment within the village of Hastings-on-the-Hudson. A suitable redevelopment of this area will benefit residents and future generations if it can become financially and environmentally sustainable.

This year, Scenic Hudson began funding support for Hastings to make new waterfront parks or upgrade existing facilities. This will provide ways for the village to commemorate the 400th anniversary of Henry Hudson's 1609 exploration of the river.

Scenic Hudson is financing $15,000 for required soil-remediation testing and a $20,000 matching grant for preliminary park design. "I'm delighted that Scenic Hudson has awarded the village these grants that will help us reclaim and restore the old quarry," said Hastings Mayor Lee Kinnally.

Meanwhile, Dobbs Ferry adopted the Local Waterfront Revitalization Program (LWRP) in August 2005. The LWRP is a plan for the local waterfront and downtown areas in Dobbs Ferry and is a guide for future enhancement, preservation, protection, and development of Dobbs Ferry's waterfront areas.

Within the LWRP is the 4.4 Water Edge project site that is located within the village of Dobbs Ferry's Waterfront Revitalization Boundary and New York State Coastal Area Boundary. The LWRP acknowledges the visual resources (such as the Hudson) and specific properties that afford views of the Hudson River. The village considers the Hudson River to be an open space, scenic resource.

Today, Dobbs Ferry is looking ahead toward its' future existence with the Hudson River as Jacqueline and David Finkelstein, both with JSF Development LLC, plan to make the eleven-home "Waters Edge" in the village a reality. This $28 million development project will become a new community showcasing eleven homes that will be located in a peaceful setting with views reaching out across the Hudson to the Palisades (area located on the Hudson River's western shoreline in northeastern New Jersey and southeastern New York).

Developers with JSF Development said they chose Dobbs Ferry because they were considering the New York City commuters. Developers stated Dobbs Ferry is an easy commute to New York City while it also provides the peace and elegance of living on the river.

In the meantime, another Ginsburg developer project was finally approved and Dobbs Ferry now plans to have 24 luxury town houses and condos built on a steep slope overlooking its waterfront park. Also in the works for Dobbs Ferry is "The Landing," a site where 104 luxury town homes and a private beach will exist near the river.

Regarding overall residential development in Dobbs Ferry, the landscaping material of future homes needs to suitably screen the new homes without blocking views of the Hudson River. Sufficient buffering is also planned to minimize visual effects of the proposed action from the Hudson River. Moreover, the utmost policy of the LWRP that must be abided by includes maintaining and enhancing Dobbs Ferry's natural areas, improving infrastructure, and implementing measures to prevent erosion and stormwater runoff into the Hudson River and its tributaries.

The village just north of Dobbs Ferry is Irvington. The village of Irvington now has Scenic Hudson Park, a relatively new 12-acre recreational facility on the Hudson River. The park offers great views of the Manhattan skyline, the Hudson River, Tappan Zee Bridge and the New Jersey Palisades. Located on the site of an old lumber yard and bus depot, this waterfront park was the first brownfields project to be financed under New York State's Clean Water/Clean Air Bond Act, a program geared at reclaiming former industrial sites. This waterfront park was a public/private initiative involving Scenic Hudson, Inc., the New York State Department of Environmental Conservation (NYSDEC) and the village of Irvington.

Besides riverside towns in Westchester County, the Village of Nyack in Rockland County (the county on the opposite side of the Hudson from Westchester) plans to redesign and expand its Nyack Memorial Park with more green space and enhanced amenities. Nyack Memorial Park offers great views of the Hudson River and is a well-known gathering place used for concerts, baseball and fishing.

Scenic Hudson, Inc. is providing $40,000 to help fund a new master plan design for the park. This plan design consists of naturalizing the shoreline, adding a fishing pier along with a rowing boathouse, and relocating parking areas away from the river's edge.

In addition to Scenic Hudson, the Nyack Park Conservancy, a local volunteer group, is supporting the village with $20,000 for long-term plans. These plans include building a deep-water dock, restoring wetlands, and removing the remains of sunken offshore barges.

"This is great for Nyack and great for the Hudson Valley. It gets us closer to our long-term goal of better connecting the village to the river," said Nyack Mayor John Shields.

Like riverside towns in Dutchess, Putnam, Westchester, Rockland, and other counties in New York State, New York City has plans to develop and redevelop its waterfront areas. In fact, there are about 20 projects in New York City now in the planning stages or are under way to develop piers overlooking the Hudson River for commercial and recreational use. The largest projects are in Manhattan and Brooklyn, although the city is looking into the Bronx and Staten Island. For example, New York City also plans to design "The Bronx - Hudson River Greenway Trail," which will be a waterfront trail that starts from Dyckman Street and extends north to Westchester County, NY.

In Manhattan, over a dozen piers, mostly on the West Side, are being redeveloped for transportation and recreational uses. For instance, developers are biding with New York City to refurbish Pier 40 on Houston Street, on land controlled by the Hudson River Park Trust. In January 2008, a proposal was made by Pier 40 Partnership (a community parent's group), for the pier to be refurbished with a bike path, a public high school, other recreational space, and new artist space. The Community Board 2's Waterfront Committee and the Pier 40 Working Group approved the plan. And the Hudson River Park Trust had a meeting about the above proposal to reach a consensus to avoid any more delays on the project.

Nonetheless, the bulk of the West Side Manhattan piers can be used only for recreational uses under the state legislation that made Hudson River Park, a 550-acre waterfront park. The park's borders encompass 34 piers from Battery Park to 59th Street, but only 13 piers are used as public space. The rest of the space is used as ferry docks, a cruise ship terminal space, and are not parts of the park. Fortunately, increased access to the waterfront has been a priority of New York Mayor Michael Bloomberg. In fact, one example of Bloomberg's initiative is taking place on Manhattan's West Harlem waterfront, As part of this project, which started in 2005, the pier at the end of 125th Street will be connected with Riverside Park and a new pier will be built for ferries to New Jersey.

As for Brooklyn, most of its pier projects focus on commercial use, with the exception of Brooklyn Bridge Park that adds more recreational space along the Downtown Brooklyn waterfront. Besides Brooklyn, the city of New York is also identifying future Hudson riverfront redevelopment sites in the Bronx. The city is now looking at about forty acres on six underused or vacant commercial sites in the Bronx that eventually can be redeveloped for residential or mixed use.

In New Jersey, from Jersey City to Fort Lee, luxury condominiums and rental apartments have been built on these riverfront communities across the Hudson from Manhattan. The apartment units that were recently constructed in Jersey City and other Hudson County cities are made up of mostly one and two-bedroom apartments with a few studio apartments. Besides residential units, many new piers are being redeveloped into waterfront parks in Hoboken, just north of Jersey City. Meanwhile, citizens of Bergen County, NJ are seeing the development of many waterfront townhouses. Today, the focus of every building along the Hudson River in New Jersey is the view of Manhattan's skyline. More New Jersey waterfront projects that are newly built or in the planning stages are Watermark, a 206-unit condo on River Road in North Bergen, and One Hudson Park, the first new high-rise condominium to be erected in Edgewater. Edgewater is just across the river from New York's Upper West Side and Harlem.

Although commercial and residential waterfront development along the Hudson River is crucial to boost the overall economy, it also helps protect the river's scenery. With waterfront revitalization projects, residents and visitors can continue to enjoy Hudson River views.

For over one hundred years, New York State has acted to preserve many of the Hudson River Valley's most breathtaking, picturesque, features. These features are the Palisades (scenic cliffs on Hudson's West Bank across from New York City), Hudson Highlands (area where Bear Mountain Park lies), and the view of the Catskill Mountains (northern New York). The continued development of waterfront revitalization projects (riverside houses, condos, shops, restaurants, etc.) will enhance viewing opportunities so people can appreciate the river's scenery. And as the state acts to improve the water quality of the Hudson River itself, riverside property values will continue to increase.

Yet despite many people supporting the development of commercial and residential buildings to be erected on the Hudson River, Kathryn Wasserman Davis, a 100-year-old woman who kayaked for many years on the Hudson, opposes property development on the river. In fact, on June 15, 2007, Wasserman Davis, a true Hudson River lover, pledged $20 million to Scenic Hudson to help save the river's banks from residential and commercial real estate development.

The gift from Davis to Scenic Hudson will now allow the New York State-based conservation organization to buy land along the Hudson that might otherwise be purchased for commercial or housing use. The money will not be transferred to Scenic Hudson until Davis dies, but Scenic Hudson plans to put her donation to use before then by borrowing against it. The group plans to use the money to speed up its land-purchasing program. It also plans to build new parks and preserves that will provide views of the Hudson River, as well as areas for hiking and other recreational activities.

In addition to waterfront developments, the Hudson River Valley real estate market for potential buyers is good and bad. According to real estate agents in Hudson Valley, good news for buyers are that across the Hudson Valley, there are a lot more homes on the market than there have been in recent years. Real estate brokers claim that sellers have been pricing their properties more realistically.

The bad news is that even buyers with a million dollars to spend often have to make compromises on the country home of their dreams. Dutch settlers who built those 18th century farmhouses tended to place them close to the road or didn't design their layouts with a modern, open floor plan in mind. More bad news is that if you are not affluent, it is very difficult for middle-class people to afford single-family homes on the Hudson, especially if the homes come with picturesque, riverside views.

In Westchester County, many people are now buying condos on the Hudson River. Realtors claim that one reason why the public likes condos is that some aren't as pricey as Westchester's single-family homes. In Ossining, developers are now working on One Harbor Square, a seven-story luxury complex along the Hudson River.

Like Westchester County, Dutchess County is near New York City and real estate for single-homes there is also pricey. "If you are after a house that sits in the countryside and it has some ambiance, it's pretty tough to find anything under half a million dollars anymore," said Kevin Battistoni, a real estate broker based in Millbrook, NY. "Nicely restored houses on more acreage with a view push a million dollars or more."

So as prices skyrocketed in Westchester and Dutchess counties and properties with acreage became scarcer, home purchasers began migrating north into Columbia County, which is located between the Hudson River and Massachusetts. "The further north you go, you end up getting more land or a bigger house and pay less money," said Mr. Freed, a Realtor with the Kinderhook Group based in Dutchess County. Freed recently sold an 18th-century, six-bedroom Dutch farmhouse on ten acres with a view of the Catskills for just $375,000.

Across the river from Columbia County, Greene County has more bargains than either of its neighboring counties, because it's farther from New York City. Freed said that in Catskill, a popular town on the west side of the Hudson, you can buy a very handsome house for $250,000 to $300,000. Other more affordable homes can be found near Livingston Manor in Sullivan County. Realtors stated that people could buy a two-bedroom cabin, vacation home near Livingston, overlooking a valley in the Catskills, for under $200,000.

Meanwhile in New Jersey, new condominium homes are being built in Hoboken on the Hudson River waterfront. These condos comprise what is now known as the development, "Maxwell Place on the Hudson." According to local real estate agents in North Jersey, Maxwell Place is a great place for singles over 30 to live in. Also it gives homeowners the best in convenient, elegant and urban living. From a Maxwell Place condominium in New Jersey, you can see Manhattan from a panoramic perspective. The condo skyline lights up at night and serves as the ideal backdrop for the beauty of the Hudson River and your Hoboken condominium. Hence, once in a Maxwell condo, you can enjoy Manhattan from your living room window or in minutes, you can be right in the heart of New York City.

As for New York State and regards to its overall economy, there's no doubt that the economy of the Hudson River Valley and the state benefit when the Hudson River is clean and in good health. The region's economy also benefits when the Hudson Valley's real estate market is thriving and communities along the river improve, revitalize and/or develop each of their waterfront areas. In addtion, the economy of each community in New Jersey, which lies on the Hudson River, will also reap the benefits from what I just mentioned.

Chapter 6
Some Historical Highlights of the Hudson River and Its Valley

    Without question, what sets the Hudson apart from other rivers is its rich history. Regarding more recent history, in 1980, the Hudson River Maritime Museum was founded by members of the National Maritime Historical Society, local historians, and the Steamship Alexander Hamilton Society. In 1964, Cornell Steamboat Company went bankrupt. In the early 20th century, the Cornell Steamboat Co. was at its peak and dominated Hudson River towing. However, the company didn't keep up with future social and industrial changes that occurred on the river during the 1940s and '50s. So unfortunately by '64, it was gone forever. In 1948, the Hudson River Day Line entered bankruptcy. What once was the most famous steamboat company on the Hudson, it ceased operations in '48. But fortunately, today we have another company, the "New Hudson Day Line," that continues to take passengers round-trip from New York Harbor to Bear Mountain, NY on weekends.

    Going further back in Hudson River history during the early 1900s, the village of Saugerties, NY was the ideal location on the Hudson for people who harvested ice from the river. In fact, the ice industry boomed during the early 1900s and late 1800s. That was the period when icehouses operated in the New York State towns of Malden and Glasco.

    However, the early 1900s also represented an era when New York State began to lose its close relationship with the Hudson River. Due to the industrial boom, plants, factories, and other industrial businesses started to use the Hudson as a power source, an easy and cheap way to dispose of industrial waste.

    Although this boosted the economy in the area, the river soon became very polluted. Furthermore, commercial riverboat traffic had declined in the 1930s when railroads became the river's fastest and most efficient mode of commercial and passenger transportation. The railroads brought the demise of steamboat travel and canals as rail transportation encouraged population growth and suburbanization. During the '30s, straight-line train tracks continued to be built which reconfigured the Hudson River's natural curves. Thus the Hudson landscape was changed to accommodate railroads and people were cut off from the river.

Nevertheless, before the river was plagued with pollution and steam-engine trains replaced steamboats, affluent New York businessmen started to purchase property in the Hudson River Valley for weekend and summer retreats during the mid-1800s (period when the mid-Hudson region was called "Millionaires Row"). Just to name a few millionaires, Union Pacific Railroad President Edward H. Harriman, National City Bank President James Stillman, and U.S. Senator Hamilton Fish once resided in that area.

In addition to the rich living in riverside homes, during the mid and late-1800s, steamships were very popular vessels that navigated the Hudson. As New York City grew, the steamship business boomed during the Industrial Revolution. Cargo ships also hauled everything from cement, coal, and brick to hay, ice, and oil. These were all the necessities to help New York City expand, and thus the Hudson became the important transportation link for carrying them.

In 1861, Steamboat Mary Powell was built and it sailed on the Hudson for more than 55 years. Mary Powell was one of the fastest, reliable and attractive steamboats of her time. Her schedule was to depart Kingston, NY early in the morning, make stops at Poughkeepsie, Milton, Newburgh and Cornwall, arriving in lower Manhattan during the late morning. On the return trip, Powell would leave New York in the late afternoon and arrive in Kingston in the early morning. With the help of steamboats, many riverfront towns like Newburgh and Kingston boomed as well due to this major industrialization. Over 100 ferry routes have come and gone on the Hudson as ferry service peaked in the early 1900s.

Ferries on the Hudson River played a crucial role in America's war for independence and formed communities along the river. In 1850, there were about 150 steamboats that made their way up and down the Hudson. The steamboats also fostered the invention of the steam engine, transported millions of immigrants on their first leg of their journey west, and in their last years, ferries became luxury boats that were once called "floating palaces."

Yet of the many Hudson River steamboat lines that operated on the river during the mid to late-1800s, the Hudson River Day Line was known to be the most prominent and dependable. Their steamboats were well known for speed and elegance as they provided passengers with the most enjoyable way to travel the Hudson River. Back then, the only way for people to properly see the Hudson River was from the deck of a Day Liner steamboat.

Prior to the heydays of the Day Liner and other steamboats, the first steamboats constructed for business on the Hudson River were the Clermont, Robert Fulton, FireFly, Paragon, and the Lady Richmond. Two inventors, Robert Fulton and Robert L. Livingston, owned these five steamboats. In fact, on August 14, 1807, Robert Fulton finished the first voyage of his newly constructed steamboat, the Clermont, by traveling at a speed of 5 mph on a 32-hour trip from New York City to Albany. Fulton's trip marked the start of the Industrial Revolution. Also during that period, the North River sloop (vessel with only one mast) was originally built.

During the early 1800s, steamboats and the industrialization of the Hudson River began to thrive. Manufacturing was a significant part of the Hudson's economy and most of it was driven by the needs of New York City and was facilitated by the ease of river transport.

Early manufacturing industries along the river consisted of gristmills, lumbering, sawmills, and paper mills. Brownstone from Palisades, NJ was used for construction of New York City houses and bluestone from Catskills, NY was used to pave the city's streets. In addition, steamboat-building facilities operated in New York towns such as Nyack, Newburgh and Rondout.

Cold Spring, NY blossomed to become one of the biggest and most modern iron foundries in America. Beginning after the War of 1812, the West Point Foundry benefited from reliable transportation that included the Erie Canal, Hudson River and railroads, its proximity to the Armament expertise at West Point, and natural resources (trees for charcoal, steam water to drive the bellows & iron). The Foundry manufactured the first all-iron ship in the nation, the motor for the first American-made locomotive, and the Parrot gun, a cannon that helped with the Union's victory in the Civil War. In 1831, the West Point Foundry provided the Mohawk and Hudson Railroad with the Locomotive De Witt Clinton. This rail line connected Albany with the eastern end of the Erie Canal. Yet in addition to industry, houses of worship also marked the Hudson River Valley's history during the early 19th century. In fact, The Chapel of Our Lady, which overlooks the river, was first built in 1833 as a Catholic Church for the foundry workers who migrated there from Europe.

Other manufacturing industries that flourished on the Hudson River were cement making (which used local limestone deposits), leather tanning (based in the Catskills with its abundant water and cedar trees that were used to make the dye), and ice harvesting (then a huge business). The icehouse at Barrytown, NY, owned by the Mutual Benefit Ice Company, held 60,000 tons of ice and the Knickerbocker Ice Company, which cut ice from Rockland Lake in Rockland County, employed about 3,000 people.

In addition to the Industrial Revolution, the Hudson River also played a role during the Revolutionary War Period. General George Washington relocated his headquarters to Newburgh, NY in 1782, where he remained there until the end of the Revolutionary War. The headquarters in Newburgh was used as part of Americans' defense of the Hudson Highlands from the British.

In 1778, Americans fortified West Point, NY while Fort Clinton and Fort Montgomery had been erected near Bear Mountain. Another fort, Fort Constitution, was located across the river from West Point. What also occurred during 1778 was the making of the "Great Chain" that was placed across the Hudson River. Anchored to the shore by large blocks of stone and wood, the chain was attached to logs and floated out into the river, where it ran between West Point and Constitution Island. The idea of the chain was to prevent British warships from sailing up the Hudson from New York City. However, after being found as a British spy, Benedict Arnold, who served under George Washington, escaped at Garrison, NY across the river from West Point. Nonetheless, the Americans captured the British officer who tried to take the American plans he received from Arnold to British headquarters in White Plains. Yet regardless of what happened, overall the "Great

Chain" was never tested, as no British warship made it that far up the river after it was created.

Reflecting on another date that mentions the Hudson River in American history was July 4, 1776. That was when Alexander Hamilton of the Continental Congress commanded an artillery post in New York. Then eight days later, two British battleships went into the Hudson River and sprayed lower Manhattan with cannonballs. Hamilton, then Lieutenant Colonel under General George Washington, and Continental soldiers returned fire. Hamilton, also known as an excellent writer, served until the Revolutionary War ended seven years later.

Yet besides Hamilton's role and although events that happened in the Hudson Highlands during the Revolutionary War were not the war's most decisive ones, it remained a region in which the Americans and British gave much of their attention to. Hence in 1775, the Americans fortified the Hudson Highlands, protecting the river used to transport supplies and troops. If the British had succeeded in gaining control of the Hudson, it would have broken apart the American military.

Moreover, in addition to Fulton's accomplishments with Hudson River steamships in the early 1800s and the Revolutionary War that began in 1777, the Erie Canal represented a huge part of the Hudson River's past. During the early 1800s and late 1700s, many Americans wanted a canal that would traverse the Appalachian Mountains. A canal would provide industrialists and farmers fast travel and less expensive shipping costs than by wagons over land. Then in 1817, construction of the 363-mile Erie Canal began. The whole canal, which linked the Hudson with the Great Lakes as well as the Atlantic Ocean, opened in 1825. The canal had 83 locks to raise canal boats to about 600 feet, which is the difference in altitude between Lake Erie and the Hudson River. Thus the Erie Canal also helped establish New York as a top world center for trade.

Three years after the Erie Canal was built, the Delaware & Hudson (D & H) Canal, a 108-mile canal, opened in 1828. The D & H Canal was constructed so navigators on canal boats could transport hard coal from mines in northeastern Pennsylvania to factories and markets (specifically to ports of New York) on the Hudson River. Joining Honesdale, Pennsylvania with Rondout, NY on the Hudson just south of Kingston, NY, the Delaware & Hudson Canal allowed coal to be easily hauled to New York City, where it was used for heating. The Delaware and Hudson Canal was the first canal in America built as a private enterprise. Thanks to the D & H Canal, new industries (glass works, boat builders, etc.) and towns emerged along the canal. In addition, previous industries (stone quarries, paper mills, lumber mills, etc.) improved economically by being close to a main transportation link provided by the D & H Canal.

Also during the early 1800s, artists first became attracted to the Hudson River and traveled to it as they admired its shoreline and scenery. In fact, on the same year the Erie Canal was completely built, Thomas Cole, a young artist, came to the Hudson Valley. In 1825, Cole made his first trip up the Hudson River to Catskill, NY where he immediately became infatuated by the scenery and began a stretching trip throughout the Hudson Valley. Soon after, his paintings celebrating nature launched other artists to do the same and their style became known as the "Hudson River School of Painting," which helped make the area a popular place for tourists. The 19th-century marked the heyday of the Hudson River School as many famous landscape painters studied geology. Besides Cole, founder of the Hudson River School, other artists such as Frederic Church, Asher Durand, Thomas Moran, Sanford Gifford, and others had participated in geological surveys and collected fossils.

Besides American artists, French artist Jacques Milbert took a tour of the Hudson River region in the 1820s and compiled some colored drawings of views he experienced on his trip. After Milbert returned to Paris, he wrote a summary of his travels that was published and illustrated with lithographs of the Hudson Valley scenery. That publication introduced the beauty of the Hudson River to Europeans.

Digressing to the Hudson River School, it was founded in the early nineteenth century in New York City, at the mouth of the Hudson River. There, a group of artists like Cole, joined by poets and writers, forged the first "American" landscape vision and literary voice. That American vision and voice, which still is accepted today, was grounded in the exploration of Earth's nature. The vision was originally expressed through the beautiful historic scenery of the Hudson River Valley area, including the Catskills, accessible to all via the mighty, scenic river that gave the school its name. In fact, for the next fifty years, artists flocked to the Hudson River Valley and their popularity grew as stories about them appeared in newspapers and other publications.

In addition to the Revolutionary War that I mentioned earlier, the late 1700s earmarked a period when the brick industry along the Hudson River began to boom. Hundreds of brick-making factories operated along the river during that time and these factories lasted into the 1940s. The main center for the brick industry was in Haverstraw (in Rockland County, NY) located on the widest part on the river, where prime raw material in the rich, blue clay and a skilled workforce together made the area the brickmaking capital of the world. Other riverside communities where you would find brick yards included Croton, Peekskill, Newburgh, Beacon, Cornwall, Fishkill, Kingston, Hudson, and Catskill. In addition, brick factories were found along the river in two towns in New Jersey, specifically, Little Ferry and Hackensack.

Besides bricks, the 1700s was when the Dutch invented schooners and sloops. A schooner has two masts while a sloop has one. Both of these styles of ships were very well suited for the Hudson River or navigating inland rivers as a whole. In addition to Dutch settlers, the mid-1700s marked a period when Quakers began coming to New York State. Initially, Quakers lived on the lower Hudson River counties of Westchester and Dutchess but a few of them moved north up the Hudson to Saratoga, NY in 1775. According to historians, some Indians were observing the peaceful Quakers meeting at Saratoga in 1778 but didn't bother them at all.

As for the mid-1600s, this was a time when the Mohegan Indians, a tribe of the Mahican group, occupied both banks of the Hudson River, almost to Lake Champlain. This 17th-century era also represented the Colonial Period along the shorelines of the Hudson as Dutch settlement of the Hudson Valley began in 1629. During early Colonial times, the Hudson River was known as the North River differentiating it from the Delaware River (then known as the South River). The Colonial period was when the Hudson River Valley started to experience an influx of colonists in the area, originally known as New Amsterdam, which became part of New York, then controlled by Britain. As the quest for independence from the crown started to unfold, the Hudson River played a significant role.

In addition to colonists settling on the banks of the Hudson River, the early 1600s marked the discovery of the river. The Hudson is the first river in the United States that explorers came to, that led into the interior of our nation, because it's an unusual river. From its mouth, which is at New York City, to Albany, NY, which is 150 miles north, it's a deep water river, a fjord (a narrow inlet of the sea between cliffs or steep slopes), and further north it becomes an arm of the sea and a tidal river. The Hudson River led into our country's interior far more than other American rivers on the East Coast that the explorers first navigated to in the sixteenth and seventeenth century.

Regarding explorers, on September 12, 1609, Henry Hudson was the first European to explore the Hudson River throughout its navigable length and he left behind a detailed description of his voyage. When Hudson, an Englishman, saw the river he was at the area of what now is called New York City. Hudson and his ship, the 85-foot Half Moon, along with a crew of twenty English and Dutch sailors, explored the Hudson from New York Harbor north to what is now Albany, NY. After discovering the river, Hudson called it the "River of Mountains."

Hudson was an explorer, navigator and sea captain. He was already a popular explorer of Artic waters when in 1608 Hudson was hired by the Dutch East India Company, a Dutch trading company, to find a magical, northeast, all-water route to Asia. Hudson explored the Artic and the North American coast. Hudson's explorations led to the area first being settled by the Dutch.

Historians stated that early maps and sailing journals indicate the terrain that Hudson explored was viewed as inhospitable, with poisonous snakes and wild animals that were found all over the area. Also, thick forests and mountains were there which made the area too dense to traverse. The Hudson River itself was seen as dangerous, especially in the stretch known as Hudson Highlands. This area starts about fifty miles north of New York City and extends for about fifteen miles, between what is now Peekskill and Newburg. Historians claimed that this region was where hills rose up over 1,000 feet along either shore and strong winds and currents made sailing very difficult and dangerous. These areas of the Hudson River were labeled by Dutch sailors as World's End and Devil's Horse Race. Nonetheless, Henry Hudson discovered three waterways that were later named after him. They include the Hudson River, the Hudson Bay in Canada and the Hudson Strait. Furthermore, before Hudson explored the three Hudson-related bodies of water that I just mentioned, he is also credited with the discovery of the shoreline of Delaware (today the area is known as the Delaware River & Delaware Bay located along the states of Delaware, Maryland, New Jersey and Pennsylvania).

    Just prior to Hudson's voyage and discovery in the early 1600s, French explorer Samuel de Champlain discovered a nearly complete water route from the St. Lawrence River to the Hudson River. And over eighty years before the expeditions by Hudson and Champlain were finished, Giovanni da Verrazano, a Florentine explorer employed by King Francis I of France, is believed to be the first white man to have seen and noted the mouth of the Hudson River in 1524. Of course, American Indians had already settled along the Hudson River before Hudson, Champlain and Verrazano arrived. Popular tribes that resided by the river until the end of the 17th century were the Mahicans and Mohawks before the Iroquois Indians began to settle in the region. Furthermore, according to some scientists, archeologists, researchers and historians, the Hudson River Valley was originally settled at about 10,000 BC by Native Americans that were attracted by its abundance.

Author's Summary

When I conducted my research on the Hudson River and Hudson Valley, I found a wealth of information on the subject. In fact, there's so much information that I found on this topic, that no author could completely put all of it into one book. That's why there are different authors who focused on different aspects of the Hudson River. My book, "Hudson River," will give readers an overall picture and education of what the Hudson River, one of America's most popular rivers, is all about.

The Hudson River estuary is one of New York State's treasured natural resources, known for its scenery and history throughout the world. The river has been and remains one of New York State's top natural assets and is a vital engine of the state's economy. It also attracts tourist dollars, provides high quality residential and commercial development, sustains multi-million dollar coastal fisheries, and it's a crucial transportation link in the state's import and export economy.

In addition, environmentalists, scientists, New York State officials, and others have divided the Hudson estuary into three regions: the Upper Hudson, Mid-Hudson, and Lower Hudson. The Upper Hudson River area is mainly rural and agricultural, with some urbanized sections near the cities of Troy, Rensselaer, and Albany. The Mid-Hudson River area is more suburbanized than the Upper Hudson area and the Lower Hudson River area is predominately urbanized.

The Upper Hudson area is geared toward dairy farming and agriculture. Yet the industrial part of this area ranges from basic manufacturing to research, development-oriented businesses and high technology. The Upper Hudson area also supports granaries, refineries, and paper mills. Regarding sports and recreation, the Upper Hudson region offers people swimming, skiing, camping, fishing, boating, and hiking.

The Mid-Hudson area has a very diversified economy that focuses on electronics, pharmaceuticals, business services, distribution, and tourism. The area's top private employers consist of manufacturing, services, and retailers. This region also supports a big presence of engineers, chemists, scientists and computer programmers who work in many industrial research laboratories in that area. As for recreation and sports, the Mid-Hudson region offers many recreational opportunities such as Catskill Park and many big state parks. The Catskill region has many huge year-round resorts and skiing, golf, hiking, and water sports are popular there. The area also offers the public an array of art galleries, museums, and historical attractions.

Finally, New York City controls the Lower Hudson area's economy. New York City's economy is led by the financial and health service industries. The city of New York also leads our country when it comes to apparel manufacturing, accounting, communications, and insurance. Tourism, foreign travel, and the export industry also have a tremendous impact on New York City's economy. From Central Park to Broadway to Herald Square, the city offers visitors theater, music, sports, arts, special events, shopping, sightseeing, historic sites, skyscrapers (that come with observation decks), and many other activities and attractions.

Regarding the entire river, almost one-third of New York State residents live within an hour's drive of the Hudson River. The whole river area also benefits from a diversified economic base and from many opportunities in housing, culture, recreation and education. Overall, the Hudson River continues to be a significant part of the lives and lifestyles of New York as well as New Jersey residents.

The Hudson is also one of the nation's only navigable passages through the Appalachian Mountains and is an important link between the Atlantic Ocean and tbe Great Lakes. The river supports deep-draft traffic from the Battery (lower Manhattan) all the way to the Port of Albany, NY and barge traffic north of Albany through a series of dams and locks to Fort Edward, NY.

The Hudson River sets itself apart from other rivers in that it is a diversified mix of swamps, marshes, and flats that span a range of salt influence from seawater to freshwater. These habitats are the heart of the ecosystem, playing a significant role as nursery grounds for fish and shellfish species, nesting sites, and migration stop areas for birds and sources of nutrients to the food chain. Today, protecting the Hudson River estuary as integrated estuarine system benefits plants, insects, birds, wildlife, and us as human beings. Other benefits that a healthy ecosystem provides includes water supply, navigation and sustainable community growth.

Nowadays, improved water quality in the Hudson Estuary has made it possible for people to enjoy the river in a lot of ways, including fishing and even swimming.

The entire Hudson River is utilized for recreational boating and you can see many recreational as well as commercial boats navigate the Hudson. From canoes to sailboats to tugboats and barges, the mighty Hudson accommodates all of these vessels. Besides boats, whether it's fish, birds or reptiles, you will always find a variety of wildlife in and near the river. And if you enjoy hiking and other recreational activities, there's always something to see and do in, on, or by the Hudson. Overall, the Hudson River is a major transportation link to world trade, enhances the northeast region's economy, and provides a variety of life forms with suitable habitats and a diverse ecology. It also offers us picturesque scenery, ancient geology, and an interesting, long history. My book will educate readers on what the Hudson River was, is and where it may be headed; especially when it comes to global warming and river cleanup efforts made by the state of New York, Environmental Protection Agency (EPA) and other entities joining together to keep it clean.

As for keeping the river clean and fighting to protect it, Christopher Swain went way beyond what conservationists and environmentalists have ever done to maintain the health of the Hudson. In fact, Swain risked his life so he could prove to everyone how important the Hudson River is to him. So on July 28, 2004, Swain, a swimmer and photographer, swum the whole length of the river. Despite PCB contamination, hydroelectric dams, sewage, and snapping turtles, Swain became the first person to swim the entire length of the Hudson River from the Adirondack Mountains to New York City.

Although I wouldn't swim in the Hudson unless it was in a designated beach area, like Swain, I have a place in my heart for the Hudson River. For me, the Hudson brings back memories of Dobbs Ferry, a Hudson River village in Westchester County, NY, where I was raised. But what I find to be of more importance is how the river is an important natural resource of the area's plants, fish, wildlife, and entire ecosystem as well as for the residents of New York and New Jersey. Yet its importance doesn't stop there; the Hudson indirectly and directly affects other rivers, water bodies, ecosystems, Americans, and even people throughout the world!

My research on the Hudson educated me on the river and I sincerely hope that it will give you, the reader, a better idea of how important this special river is on a local, national, and international level. And although the length of the Hudson River isn't as long as the Mississippi River, its past is just as long and it does have a unique place in world history. Moreover, the Hudson's role within our global ecosystem is just as important as the role the Mississippi and other rivers play.

To many people, the Hudson is a mystical, mighty and magnificent river. For me, it's a huge river that will always flow in my mind because it flowed near my school and home. Moreover, on June 21, 1980, my high school graduation ceremony was conducted at Dobbs Ferry's Waterfront Park on the Hudson. And of course, I will always recall those hot and sizzling summer days when my brother, Joe Bernardo, and I caught and enjoyed the Hudson's fish and blue crabs. Finally, there's one other reason that motivated me to write my book on the Hudson River; that's words from a song I listened to many times that is sung by Billy Joel. My favorite part of Joel's New York-theme song is: "I'm just taking a Greyhound up the Hudson River Line, cause I'm in a New York state of mind!"

About the Author

John Bernardo is the published author of five books. John's last book was a non-fiction one which was about the Delaware River. His book on the Delaware was published in January, 2013.

Bernardo became a freelance reporter and writer in 1988. He has an impressive writing background that consists of more than 500 articles (some for magazines, the rest in newspapers) that were published under his byline.

John's interests include visiting railroad museums, visiting nature centers and playing miniature golf. Born and raised in Westchester County, New York, John currently resides in Miami, Florida with his wife, Agustina and two daughters, Michelle and Melissa.

www.ingramcontent.com/pod-product-compliance
Lightning Source LLC
Chambersburg PA
CBHW050642160426
43194CB00010B/1778